P9-BTO-998

WITHDRAWN

WITHDRAWN

Malaysia

Malaysia

BY SYLVIA McNAIR

Enchantment of the World
Second Series

139423

Children's Press®

A Division of Scholastic Inc.

NEW YORK TORONTO LONDON AUCKLAND SYDNEY
MEXICO CITY NEW DELHI HONG KONG
DANBURY, CONNECTICUT

Frontispiece: Kite maker at work

Consultant: Dr. Sumit Ganguly, professor of Asian Studies and Government, the University of Texas at Austin

Please note: All statistics are as up-to-date as possible at the time of publication.

Book production by Herman Adler Design

Library of Congress Cataloging-in-Publication Data

McNair, Sylvia
    Malaysia / by Sylvia McNair.
      p. cm. — (Enchantment of the world. Second series)
    Includes bibliographical references and index.
    ISBN 0-516-21009-2
    1. Malaysia—Juvenile literature. [1. Malaysia.] I. Title. II. Series.
  DS592.M395   2002
  959.5—dc21
    meN
                         2001047738

© 2002 by Children's Press, a Division of Scholastic Inc.
All rights reserved. Published simultaneously in Canada.
Printed in the United States of America.

CHILDREN'S PRESS and associated logos are trademarks and or registered
trademarks of Grolier Publishing Co., Inc. SCHOLASTIC and associated logos
are trademarks and or registered trademarks of Scholastic Inc.
1 2 3 4 5 6 7 8 9 10 R 11 10 09 08 07 06 05 04 03 02

BROCKWAY MEMORIAL LIBRARY
10021 N.E. 2nd AVENUE
MIAMI SHORES. FLA. 33138

Acknowledgments

The author is very grateful to staff members of Malaysia Tourism for their help in making it possible to see the highlights of Malaysia firsthand, answering questions, and arranging my itinerary and personal interviews. Special thanks go to Raja Normelaa, Alice Scully, and Syaliza Azia. Also, the friendly and helpful attention of my guide, Linggam, and driver, Remmy, made the on-site research most enjoyable. Helena Zukowsky, who lived in Malaysia for many years, shared many of her source materials with me, and I thank her. To Anna Idol, thanks once again for your work on the final manuscript. Any errors that may have crept into the book in spite of the assistance of these people are the responsibility of the author.

Contents

Cover photo:
Dunsun harvest
dancers

CHAPTER

Borneo rain forest

Traditional dancers

Selamat Pagi ("Good Morning")

Young faces of Malaysia

Malaysia is an amazing coun-
try. It is amazing that it is a country at all.
How did such a diverse group of people get
together and form a united nation? The
population of Malaysia includes dozens
of ethnic groups who speak different
languages or dialects. Some people live
in small *kampungs*, or villages where they
make their living by farming or fishing.
Some are employed in large, modern cities. Some Malaysian
states were small kingdoms until only a few years ago. In others,
authority was mostly in the hands of village chiefs.

Malaysia is made up of two distinct regions, separated by
about 400 miles (644 kilometers) of the South China Sea. One
of these regions occupies a long, narrow peninsula in Southeast
Asia. The other shares a large island with two other nations.

Malaysia is an old country with a very young face. The
people of Malay descent, who make up a little more than half
of the total population, have a long history, but the nation of
Malaysia has existed for less than fifty years. Traders and travelers have visited port cities of Malaysia for hundreds of years,
yet jungles and forests exist in interior regions that are still
almost unknown to the rest of the world.

These contrasts and contradictions are what make
Malaysia such a fascinating country to visit. In Kuala Lumpur,

Opposite: **Dawn on a West
Malaysian beach**

The Petronas Twin Towers dominate Kuala Lumpur's skyline.

A colorful Buddhist temple

the capital city, you will see the tallest building in the world. The Petronas Twin Towers are a symbol of what modern Malaysians have accomplished. Shiny coils of stainless steel glow in the sunlight and glitter as evening lights are turned on. They rise up and up to pierce the clouds and overlook the city below. Several other important buildings constructed during the 1990s proclaim Kuala Lumpur a city of the future. Mixed with the new structures are sultans' palaces, Moorish mosques, and buildings reminiscent of the country's British colonial past. There are also temples—Hindu temples with ornate carvings from Indian lore, Chinese temples easily recognized by their shapes and brilliant colors.

You'll discover that the very latest in technology is available in Malaysia. You'll also find rural people who live much the same way that their ancestors did.

Even more diverse than the lifestyles, languages, and ethnic backgrounds of the people are the plants and animals in this small tropical country. There are flowers as large as a room and others as small as a fingernail. Some birds wall themselves up inside a tree while nesting. Extraordinary fireflies turn on and off in unison.

Some of the world's largest caves and loveliest beaches are in Malaysia.

Are you ready to explore? Come along. Malaysia is ready to greet you.

Geopolitical map of Malaysia

A Tropical Paradise

A beach on Sibu Island

Opposite: **The Segama River winds through a rain forest in Borneo.**

"THE MOON HAS FALLEN INTO MY LAP," HUGH CLIFFORD, a young man from England, wrote in his diary in 1887. He was describing how happy he felt about the news that he would be working in the Malay Peninsula. He loved the beauty of this tropical region.

The term "Malay" has been used for several hundred years. The Malay Peninsula is a strip of land in southeastern Asia, south of Thailand. The largest ethnic group of people here are known as Malays. And the Malay Archipelago is a very large group of islands south of the peninsula. Several countries are spread out on these islands.

Malaysia, on the other hand, is a newer name. It was given to a new nation, formed from a federation of several former colonies and kingdoms in 1963.

Geographical Features

Highest Elevation: Mount Kinabalu, 13,431 feet (4,094 m) above sea level

Lowest Elevation: Sea level, along the coast

Longest Rivers: Rajang and Kinabatangan Rivers, 350 miles (563 km) long

Greatest Average Annual Precipitation: 150 inches (381 cm) in Sarawak and Sabah

Lowest Average Annual Precipitation: 100 inches (254 cm) on the Malaysian Peninsula

Hottest Average Temperature: 90°F (32°C) along the coasts

Lowest Average Temperature: 55°F (13°C) in the mountains

Longest Shared Border: With Indonesia, 1,107 miles (1,782 km)

Greatest Length: 670 miles (1,078 km) in East Malaysia

Greatest Width: 240 miles (386 km) in East Malaysia

Coastline: 2,905 miles (4,675 km) long

World's Tallest Building: Petronas Twin Towers in Kuala Lumpur, 1,483 feet (452 m) high

World's Largest Cave: Sarawak Chamber in Gunung Mula National Park, 2,300 feet (701 km) long, 980 feet (299 km) wide, and 230 feet (70 km) high

Size and Location

The country of Malaysia has an unusual shape and location. It consists of two parts, separated by a large stretch of the South China Sea. West Malaysia is the portion on the Malay Peninsula. East Malaysia is on a large island named Borneo.

The Malay Peninsula is a long, narrow strip of land that extends southward from the southeastern corner of Asia.

Marshy lowlands of West Malaysia

Two countries share this peninsula. The northern portion, quite long and slim, is part of Thailand. The southern, wider part, is West Malaysia. The peninsula is about 200 miles (322 km) across at its widest point. Singapore is a small independent nation located on an island at the southern tip of the peninsula.

East Malaysia is 400 miles (644 km) away, across the South China Sea, on the large island of Borneo. Three nations share this island—Malaysia, Brunei, and Indonesia. Malaysia's section lies along the northern coast of the island.

All together, Malaysia occupies an area of 128,525 square miles (332,878 square kilometers). Of this total area, about 60 percent is in East Malaysia, 40 percent in West Malaysia.

The country of Thailand is West Malaysia's northern neighbor. Singapore is on the southern border of West Malaysia. In East Malaysia, between the states of Sarawak and Sabah on the northeastern coast of the island of Borneo, is the tiny nation of Brunei. About two-thirds of the island of Borneo, south of both Sarawak and Sabah, belongs to the Indonesian state of Kalimantan.

States and Territories

Malaysia is divided into thirteen states and two federal territories. Every state in both sections of the nation overlooks the sea. Eleven of the states and part of the Federal Territory are on the peninsula. From north to south, on the west side, are the states of Perlis, Kedah, Pulau Pinang, Perak, Selangor, Negeri Sembilan, and Melaka. Wilayah Persekutuan, in which the capital city of Kuala Lumpur is located, is part of the Federal Territory. It lies between Selangor and Negeri Sembilan. On the east, facing the South China Sea, are Kelantan, Terengganu, Pahang, and Johor. The states of Perlis, Kedah, Perak, and Kelantan are all on the northern border of peninsular Malaysia.

The two states of Sarawak and Sabah, and Labuan, part of the Federal Territory, are in East Malaysia. Labuan, off the northeastern tip of Sarawak, is a duty-free island. That means that goods are imported from other parts of the world and sold on the island without an additional customs charge.

Looking at Malaysia's Cities

Ipoh, Malaysia's second-largest city, is the capital of the state of Perak. It lies on both banks of the Kinta River in the tin-mining area of the Kinta Valley. Founded in the 1880s by rich Chinese miners, the city today remains under the influence of its founders' descendants. Surrounding Ipoh are limestone formations with many cave temples, including Perak Tong Temple and Sam Poh Tong Temple, that honor Buddha. Malaysia's only geological museum is also in the city.

Johor Baharu, Malaysia's third-largest city, is the capital of the state of Johor. The city is linked to the country of Singapore to the south by a causeway. Founded by a former sultan of Melaka in the 1500s, the city today is an important Malaysian commercial center. Recently, banks, industrial parks, shopping centers, and hotels have been built. Tourists enjoy visiting the Istana Besar (pictured below), once the palace for the sultans and now a museum. Another important landmark is the Sultan Abu Bakar Mosque, which can hold more than 2,000 worshipers.

Melaka is the country's fourth-largest city and the capital of the state of Melaka. Founded in 1400 by the Malay prince Paramesvara, the city has been controlled by the Portuguese, the Dutch, and the British at various times in history. Under each of these groups, Melaka was an important trading center. The old part of the city still has churches, public buildings, and shops that were built by the Europeans. Many descendants from early Chinese traders live in Melaka's Chinatown. Today, Melaka is a great city for shopping. Many shopping malls have recently been built.

Petaling Jaya, Malaysia's fifth-largest city, is a fast-growing suburb southwest of Kuala Lumpur. Starting as a place for workers in Kuala Lumpur to live, this suburb is now an important industrial center. Many high-tech companies have moved there, including some from the United States. Businesspeople can stay in Petaling Jaya's new Hilton and Hyatt hotels.

A rocky ridge towers above the rain forest.

Peninsular Malaysia

Coastal plains border the Malay Peninsula on both waterfronts, from north to south. The plains are swampy and narrow. Parading down the center of this landmass are several ranges of rather high mountains. A mountain chain actually begins far to the north, in the country of Myanmar (formerly called Burma). After extending all through the Malay Peninsula, it disappears under the ocean and is seen again in Borneo. The mountainous spine of the peninsula divides West Malaysia geographically, making travel between the east and west coasts difficult.

Rain forests cover the sides of the mountains; granite ridges tower above. Several peaks in the Titi Wangsa Range are more than 6,000 feet (1,828 meters) high; the highest, Mount Taham, has an elevation of 7,175 feet (2,187 m).

Settlements in Malaysia grew up close to rivers or to the sea. At one time, rivers provided the only means of travel through the forests. They are still important and are used for fishing, rafting, kayaking, and transportation. Most rivers on the peninsula run north to south. Most of them are not very long, and their descent from the mountains is steep. The Pahang, 295 miles (475 km) long, is the longest in West Malaysia. It flows from the northwestern part of the peninsula to the South China Sea. The Perak, 150 miles (241 km) long, has been dammed to create Lake Chenderoh, a source of hydroelectricity.

The majority of West Malaysia's inhabitants live on the western coastal plain, which is about 50 miles (80 km) wide. The east coast is a popular tourist destination for foreign visitors, especially people from Singapore. Beautiful tropical beaches face the ocean on this side of the peninsula.

The northwestern section of peninsular Malaysia includes the states of Perlis, the nation's smallest state; Kedah; Pulau Pinang; and Perak. Rice, grown in irrigated paddies, is a major crop in the far north. Rubber and oil-palm plantations cover much of the fertile land. Vegetable gardens and bright green bushes of tea blanket the rolling hillsides of the Cameron Highlands. Mist-covered hills and lively waterfalls add to the beauty of the region.

The northwestern part of the peninsula was once a major center for tin mining; today many of the mines are abandoned. The landscape is dotted with large limestone outcroppings on some parts of the mainland and many of the offshore islands. Drawings and paintings found in a cave in Perak are more than 2,000 years old.

Cameron Highlands

"A fine plateau with gentle slopes shut in by the mountains" is the way a government surveyor named William Cameron described the region that bears his name today. The Cameron Highlands are called the vegetable capital of Malaysia. The mountains that tower above the tea plantations and farms rise to more than a mile high. The beauty of the highlands and the fresh air—much cooler than at lower levels—have made the region a popular destination for hikers, college students, vacationing families, and tourists.

East Malaysia

Much of East Malaysia, on the island of Borneo, is covered with lush tropical jungles. The coastline is very irregular, cut with estuaries and scalloped with bays. Swampy lowlands give way to forested hills and lofty mountains in the interior.

In many regions, rivers are the only means of reaching inland. Most settlements have grown up beside the sea or along the rivers. Malaysia's two longest rivers are in East Malaysia—the Rajang in Sarawak and the Kinabatangan in Sabah. Each is about 350 miles (563 km) long.

Rivers are used for transportation in East Malaysia.

Sabah covers the northeastern tip of Borneo. It is dominated by the mountains of the Crocker Range. Its major rivers flow into the Sulu Sea, which lies between Borneo and the Philippine Islands.

Mount Kinabalu, the highest peak in Malaysia

Mangrove swamp in Sarawak

The lowlands of Sarawak are primarily mangrove swamps and saline (salty) swamp forests. Only one-fifth of this state has land suitable for agriculture.

Caves

Some of the world's largest and most spectacular caves are found in Sarawak, on Borneo. Gunung Mulu National Park, on the border of Brunei in northeastern Sarawak, is famous for its limestone cave formations. More than 124 miles (200 km) have been explored within the cave. Much more has not yet been mapped. Sarawak Chamber, the largest known cave room in the world, is said to be large enough to hold sixteen football fields or forty jumbo jets.

Sabah also has large caves at Gomantong, near its northeastern coast. Thousands of bats, as well as tiny birds called swiftlets, inhabit these caves.

Two locations of peninsular Malaysia are also popular with spelunkers (people who like to explore caves). Langkawi is an archipelago of 100 islands—some of them only single rocks—off northwestern Malaysia. About twenty-four caves are scattered among these islands. Taman Negera National Park, one of the world's oldest tropical rain forests, attracts visitors to fish in its streams, climb its mountains, and explore its caves.

The weather in Malaysia is constant throughout the year—nearly always wet. The two sections of the country lie within the rainfall zone just north of the equator. The country is also south of Asia's hurricane belt. Early sailing ships were put into the harbors of the Straits of Malacca to ride out frequent monsoons.

Seasons in Malaysia are described as "wet" and "very wet." Records of rainfall in 1986 show that in Kuala Lumpur, in peninsular Malaysia, more than one out of every two days had rain, a total of 185 wet days. Kuching, in East Malaysia, received even more rain than Kuala Lumpur—248 rainy days! Naturally, with this much rain, flash floods are a frequent problem.

People wading through floodwaters near Kuala Lumpur

Temperatures are usually in the 80's and 90's Farenheit (high 20's and 30's Celcius) during the daytime, dropping to the mid-70°sF (low 20°sC) at night. The highest temperature on record is 109°F (43°C). It is somewhat cooler in the mountainous regions; a low of 36°F (2°C) has been reported in the Titi Wangsa Range.

CHAPTER

THREE

A Land Teeming with Life

24

J

UST IMAGINE TRYING TO COUNT HOW MANY KINDS OF LIVING things exist in Malaysia's tropical rain forests, caves, wetlands, and ocean waters. There are animals that walk, hop, fly, slither, and swim. Some are huge creatures that roam through the trees; some are the tiny crawling creatures that live mostly in the ground. One scientist counted more than 2,000 kinds of beetles. There are more than 100 kinds of frogs and at least as many species of snakes. Don't forget the snails, the grubs, and the crabs that skitter along the seashore. Other animals live in water and create huge coral reefs.

Opposite: **Frog beetles live in the rain forest.**

Malaysian horned frogs

BROCKWAY MEMORIAL LIBRARY
10021 N.E. 2nd AVENUE
MIAMI SHORES, FLA. 33138

Scientists estimate that there are millions of species of plants and animals in Malaysia's forests—more than half of all the life forms on this planet. Thousands of species have already been catalogued in the rain forests, which are some of the oldest on earth. There are countless more not yet identified. The numbers and rich variety of life forms in this tropical land are astonishing.

Forests and Jungles

The Malay Peninsula and the smaller islands that dot the ocean between the islands of Java and Borneo were once part of an unbroken continent covered with tropical forests. Naturalists call the region, including the floor of ocean that connects those islands, Sundaland. It is a distinct geographical and climatic subregion, with many plants and animals that are found nowhere else. Borneo has more unique forms of plants and animals than the rest of the region.

About three-quarters of Malaysia's land is covered with trees. Much of this is forest. The remainder consists of plantations of rubber and palm trees. The products of these plantations—timber, rubber, and palm oil—are the backbone of the nation's economy.

Malaysia has more than 15,000 flowering plants; this may be as much as 9 percent of the world's total. It has at least 2,000 types of trees and 3,000 species of orchids. More kinds of trees are grown at the Forest Research Institute and Museum, near Kuala Lumpur, than are found in all of North America. Scientists at this research center conduct

Epiphytes cover the branches of this tree.

educational courses and work with experimental plantings, including medicinal plants.

The trunks of some tropical trees are very large in circumference, but their root structure is shallow. They put down extra roots to help them stand. In some regions the forests are so dense that they form a thick ceiling that blocks out the sun. Very little vegetation can grow on the floors of these forests, but many types of plants in the tropical jungles find unusual ways to survive. Huge lianas (tropical vines) stretch out for hundreds of feet and climb upward in the Sunda rain forest in search of sunlight. Epiphytes—sometimes called air plants— live on the branches of trees. They are parasites—they live on minerals, nutrients, and water drawn from their hosts and from the air.

A Forest Feast

On the island of Borneo, giant fig trees—both strangler fig vines and free-growing trees—bear fruit that is extremely popular with the island's wildlife population. The fruit lasts only for two weeks, but when it is about to ripen, the news spreads quickly. Hornbills (pictured) send out a call to one another to come to the feast. Soon orangutans, squirrels, civets, and many other animals and birds swarm to share the feast. The gathering is much like a crowd that rushes to sample the free food offered at a community-wide event.

The largest and strongest of these animals—the orangutan—is king of the forest. No other animal will challenge a burly male orangutan for a piece of fruit.

Smaller mammals wait for the chance to grab a bite when the larger ones are finished. During the hottest part of the day, many of the animals will take a rest and let the hornbills take over. Nocturnal animals appear after the others have gone to sleep.

Just as with human crowds, the event is an occasion for play and socializing as well as for eating. Young male hornbills show off by picking fights with each other while females watch.

After fourteen days, most of the fruit is gone. Small birds come to pick at the tiny fragments that remain. The "party" breaks up, and everyone looks forward to the next one.

One jungle parasite, the rafflesia, is the largest flower in the world. It can grow as large as 3 feet (1 m) in diameter in full bloom. It is not an attractive flower. It starts to rot almost as soon as it opens, and it looks much like dead meat. Maggots are attracted to it, and it has an unpleasant odor. In contrast to the large size of the rafflesia, some flowers are so tiny they can barely be seen with the naked eye.

Most of Malaysia's trees are hardwoods, but there are some pines. Palm trees grow near rivers and villages. Mangroves thrive in swampy coastal areas. The tallest of all tropical trees, the tualang, grows as high as 260 feet (80 m) and reaches a circumference of 10 feet (3 m) around the trunk.

Thousands of kinds of wild plants—herbs, flowers, ferns, and fungi—flourish in the rain forest. Many more species of plants, as well as species of insects and small mammals, exist in rain forests than in temperate zones.

One interesting group includes the pitcher plants. These are vegetable predators, or carnivorous plants, that devour insects. The blossom holds up to seven pints of sweet liquid. Some insects are lured inside the plants by the fragrant nectar.

Measuring a giant rafflesia

Pitcher plants attract prey with their fragrant nectar.

Others fall inside by accident. Trapped inside by the slippery walls of the flowers, they drown. The mineral-rich insect bodies become nutritious food for the plants.

Mammals

At one time, tigers, elephants, leopards, rhinoceroses, and other large mammals roamed the jungles of Southeast Asia. They were found on both the Malay Peninsula and the island of Borneo. Today, these great animals are rare and in serious danger of extinction. Bear and deer can still be found in some regions.

Smaller mammals are numerous and include tapirs, wild pigs, otters, and civet cats. About forty species of primates—apes and related mammals—live in the Sunda region. Gibbon, orangutan, loris, tarsier, langur, and macaque are just a few of the types of primates living here. Some of these are rather solitary, but macaques live in large families of as many as fifty members. The males are the disciplinarians, and the females take care of the babies and youngsters.

Orangutans are found only on Borneo. The word orangutan means "man of the forest," and they have characteristics more like those of humans than any other mammals. Two

A bearded pig

protected areas where people can go to observe these primates are the Lanjak-Entimau Orangutan Sanctuary in Sarawak and the Sepilok Orang-utan Rehabilitation Center in eastern Sabah.

Orangutans are an endangered species. Their numbers are decreasing drastically. Although it is illegal to kill, own, or export orangutans, poaching is common. Poachers capture the creatures to sell as pets or for export to foreign zoos. In addition, the forest habitats where the animals live are rapidly shrinking. Agricultural development has cleared large forest areas for palm-oil plantations, and the logging industry has wiped out still more. Huge forest fires in 1997 and 1998 killed thousands of orangutans.

Young orangutans with a ranger at Sepilok Orang-utan Rehabilitation Center

Mammals in tropical rain forests find much of their food high up in the tops of trees. Some of them have developed unusual abilities to gather food—they climb, jump, and swing from branch to branch. Others, such as bats, can fly. Certain small mammals—lizards, frogs, squirrels, and shrews, for example—do not exactly fly but glide and hop in such a way that they appear to fly.

Bats

At sunset, awestruck tourists wait in Sarawak's Gunung Mulu National Park for a most extraordinary natural event that occurs each evening, except in rainy weather. They are at the Bat Observatory, across from the entrance to Deer Cave. Deer Cave no longer has any deer. Today it is home to 10 million bats. There are more bats in Malaysia than any other mammal.

As the observers wait, they see a shadowy black ribbon beginning to form outside the opening to the cave. The flying creatures are leaving the cave in search of their dinner, which consists of fruit and a total of three tons of insects. By consuming such large quantities of food, bats help to maintaining the balance of animal life in this region.

Birds and Butterflies

Malaysia's forests, jungles, and wetlands are friendly habitats for more than 700 species of birds, both residents and migrators. Nearly three-fourths of these can be seen in Kinabalu National Park. Some fill the air with music. Others attract attention by their brilliant coloring. Still others are almost impossible to spot, because their bright green feathers blend into the jungle foliage.

On Borneo, many people traditionally believe that birds are messengers from the gods. Therefore, they believe that by observing the behavior of birds, people can learn what they should and should not do.

A beautiful green area in Kuala Lumpur is a refuge for butterflies. Some 15,000 plants in Butterfly Park form an attractive habitat for thousands of these colorful flying crea-

Sarawak's State Bird

The rhinoceros hornbill is the state bird of Sarawak. It is as large as a goose and as black as a raven. It has a fat neck, long eyelashes that look like the paste-on ones sold at cosmetics counters, and a big yellow-and-red helmetlike lump on its bill.

When a female rhinoceros hornbill prepares to lay eggs, she builds a nest inside a tree. Then she produces a kind of plaster and barricades herself inside with the nest. Her mate feeds her by pushing bits of fruit through a narrow slit in the barricade. Rhinoceros hornbills mate for life.

tures. Visitors can watch pupae become butterflies in a setting of waterfalls, tortoise ponds, and gardens. One of the most spectacular butterflies, with emerald-green markings on jet-black wings, is called Rajah Brooke's Birdwing after the famous "white rajah" of Sarawak.

Rajah Brooke's Birdwing

Mangrove swamps near the shorelines of Malaysia are half sea, half land. Slender mangrove trees have roots that reach down into swampy soil as though they were stilts. The entangled roots act as traps for debris washed downstream by rivers and brought in by tides. Mangroves tolerate both saltwater and brackish (a mixture of salt and fresh) water. The crowded jungle of mangrove roots provides a habitat for reptiles, frogs, and some types of fish. Storks, kingfishers, and other shorebirds find plenty of food—fish, crabs, and smaller organisms—in the mangrove swamps. A few monkeys like these regions, too.

In the province of Perak in West Malaysia, part of a mangrove swamp has been set aside as the Kuala Gula Bird

Birds' Nest Soup

In Sabah, some small, insect-eating birds called swiftlets live in caves. They use their own saliva to make a goo that they shape into nests (pictured). People gather these nests and export them, primarily to Hong Kong and other parts of China.

The nests themselves have very little flavor, but the Chinese have prized them for generations. They add flavorings and sometimes other ingredients to make a dish called birds' nest soup. The dish is traditionally believed to be good for people's blood. Some biochemists report that the particular protein in this product does seem to stimulate regrowth of blood cells, as well as of skin cells.

It is illegal to harvest swiftlet nests when eggs or baby birds are inside them. However, birds' nest soup is so popular in East Asia that the practice is hard to regulate.

Sanctuary. Thousands of migrating birds stop here on their way south. Other creatures that make their home here include otters, monkeys, and dolphins.

Another kind of flying creature lives among mangroves along the Selangor River, about a two-hour ride from Kuala Lumpur. People come from miles around to view the incredible performance of millions of fireflies. Local boatmen row passengers up the river, where in nearly total darkness one can see the fireflies sitting on mangroves into the far distance. The amazing thing is that all these fireflies flicker on and off in perfect synchrony. It is as though a giant switch is controlling them and keeping them all pulsating in identical rhythm.

Underwater Wonders

The waters around peninsular Malaysia and north of Borneo have an impressive ecosystem of great coral reefs of brilliant colors, beds of algae, families of sea turtles and giant clams, and technicolor displays of tropical fish. Blue and emerald waters shimmer above the undersea wonderland of pink, blue, green, red, and white living creatures.

To protect these precious natural wonders, Malaysia has established several marine parks. Activities such as anchoring boats over coral areas, littering, lighting fires on the beach, and carrying weapons that might endanger aquatic life are forbidden. People are permitted to swim, snorkel, dive, take underwater pictures, and camp on the shore. However, waterskiing, speedboat racing, and spear fishing are banned, as is collecting corals and other forms of aquatic life.

Colorful fish live in Malaysia's seas.

According to experienced divers, one of the most exciting dive spots in the world is reached from Sipadan Island, off the eastern coast of Sabah. An underwater limestone peak, only 50 feet (15 m) from the shore, offers a 2,000-foot (610-m) dive wall.

Threats to the Environment

Nature has blessed Malaysia with some of the most exciting and important ecosystems in the world. At the same time, nature itself can be blamed for some of the biggest threats to the wonderful and irreplaceable rain forests. Torrential rains,

Malaysian Nature Society

In 1940, a group of Malaysian plantation owners formed the Malaysian Nature Society to protect the country's forests and other natural assets. The society promotes knowledge, enjoyment, and protection of nature through scientific study, education, and publications. It works closely with the Department of Wildlife and National Parks, the Ministry of Science and Technology, and local organizations. The society supports environmental legislation, conducts scientific studies, runs education centers, and trains teachers.

There are five types of endangered animals in this part of the world: the rhinoceros, the tiger, the Malayan sun bear, the Asian elephant, and five species of sea turtles. The society works with other Asian organizations to protect these creatures and their habitats.

Conservation of the environment often conflicts with economic interests, however. The Malaysian government's emphasis on economic growth often causes the destruction of much of the country's flora and fauna, especially that of East Malaysia.

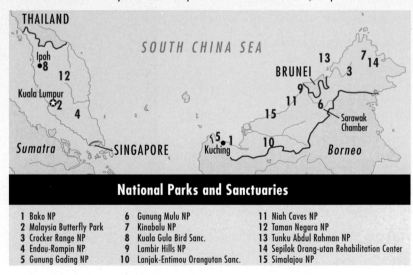

National Parks and Sanctuaries

1 Bako NP	6 Gunung Mulu NP	11 Niah Caves NP
2 Malaysia Butterfly Park	7 Kinabalu NP	12 Taman Negara NP
3 Crocker Range NP	8 Kuala Gula Bird Sanc.	13 Tunku Abdul Rahman NP
4 Endau-Rompin NP	9 Lambir Hills NP	14 Sepilok Orang-utan Rehabilitation Center
5 Gunung Gading NP	10 Lanjak-Entimou Orangutan Sanc.	15 Simalajou NP

called monsoons, pound the land, washing soil down mountainsides and into the sea. Strong winds and hot sunlight also contribute to soil erosion. However, the timber industry is an even greater threat to the future of the rain forests. Overcutting has resulted in the removal of trees off entire mountainsides. The thin and fragile soil that remains cannot support replanting, so there is no way to reverse the destruction.

One of the reasons to worry about losing rain forests is the possibility that some of the tropical plants yet to be studied or discovered may contain elements that can cure human diseases. This is a matter of concern for the whole world. But as long as other nations provide markets for more and more wood, they become part of the problem.

Warriors for the Environment is a national organization for high school students, sponsored by the Nature Society. The 165 school clubs are organized somewhat like scouting troops. Members progress through a series of programs and receive awards for completing certain activities. They work on projects at individual, community, and international levels.

Wildlife Symbols

Malaysia has no official national bird or animal at this time. The Malaysian Nature Society uses the tapir as its symbol. This rare black-and-white animal, distantly related to the rhinoceros, has a mellow disposition. Tourism Malaysia, the government tourist agency, has sometimes used the leatherback turtle as its logo. In 1996, the orangutan was the mascot of the Sixteenth Commonwealth Games, hosted in Malaysia. This "man of the forest" was chosen to symbolize that Malaysians, like orangutans, are warm, friendly, and fun.

The Malaysian Nature Society has proposed that the Malaysian peacock-pheasant (pictured), which is found only in the Malaysian Peninsula, should be chosen as the national bird.

From Ancient Kingdoms to a New Nation

Huuman settlements existed on the Malay Peninsula and the islands to the south as early as 35,000 years ago, according to archaeologists. Stone Age tools found in both West and East Malaysia are evidence of prehistoric habitation. Today's Malaysian people are descended from later waves of immigration, probably from China. One group, called Proto-Malays, arrived around 2,500 years ago. Much later, during the Iron and Bronze Ages, another group arrived. These people have been named Deutero-Malays.

Early on, this peninsula was a crossroads for travelers from far-off lands. More than 2,000 years ago, traders from India and China discovered convenient ports where they could exchange goods. In addition, the region itself was a source of valuable products, such as spices, sweet-smelling woods, and gold. Early mapmakers called the peninsula *Aurea Chersonese*, meaning the peninsula of gold.

Travelers from India influenced religion and customs throughout much of southeastern Asia. They established several trading ports in the region. Settlements built on trade began to grow and became centers of small kingdoms. From about the ninth to the thirteenth century A.D., most of the Malay Peninsula was ruled from the island of Sumatra as part of a Buddhist empire.

Opposite: **Merdeka Square commemorates Malaysia's independence.**

Hinduism and Buddhism flourished in the peninsula for about 1,500 years. Then, during the thirteenth century, Arab traders introduced a new religion, Islam.

Melaka

Melaka, on the west coast of the Malay Peninsula, was an exciting city during the 1400s and 1500s. Melaka (the English spelling is Malacca) had a fine, deep harbor and an ideal location in the Straits of Malacca, across from Sumatra on the trade routes. It was the first important port on the Malay Peninsula, and before long it became a sultanate. (Sultans are Muslim rulers of a state or a country. The title is a hereditary one, normally passed from father to son.) Lively bazaars sold all kinds of exotic goods from many lands.

Remains of a Portuguese fort in Melaka

The center of power and of social life in Melaka was the sultan's palace. The rulers converted to Islam and declared it the official religion. From Melaka, Islam and the Malay culture began to spread along the trade routes.

Portuguese and Dutch Periods

A large fleet of ships from Portugal attacked and captured Melaka in 1511. The Portuguese invaders had

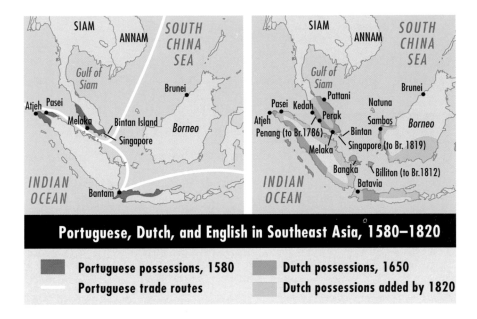

Portuguese, Dutch, and English in Southeast Asia, 1580–1820

Portuguese possessions, 1580
Portuguese trade routes

Dutch possessions, 1650
Dutch possessions added by 1820

two goals: to control the spice trade in the straits and to replace Islam with Christianity. The Portuguese occupied Melaka for more than a century but did not achieve either goal. In 1640, the United East India Company, a Dutch trading company, laid siege to Melaka. After seven months, the Dutch defeated the Portuguese.

The Dutch were more successful traders than the Portuguese had been, but they did not concentrate on Melaka. Meanwhile, several separate states were emerging on the peninsula. The states of Perak, Terengganu, and Pahang had an allegiance to the sultanate of Johor, but for the most part, they ran their own affairs. The northern states of Kelantan and Kedah were under the influence of Siam. In Borneo, Sarawak and part of Sabah were provinces of the sultanate of Brunei.

The British Arrive

The English East India Company (EIC) had had its eyes on the Malay Peninsula for some time, but its efforts were concentrated on India. In 1785, the sultan of Kedah gave the EIC permission to establish a base on the island of Pulau Pinang. This was the first step toward colonizing the peninsula. A few years later Thomas Stamford Raffles, a representative of the EIC, started another British settlement, on the island of Singapore. A treaty with the Dutch in 1824 gave the British a third spot, Melaka. The three ports—Pulau Pinang, Singapore, and Melaka—were united under British rule and named the Straits Settlements.

Sir Thomas Stamford Raffles

The British tried to stay out of internal affairs on the Malay Peninsula, but British merchants in the Straits Settlements wanted help. The Malay states held attractive investment opportunities, and the Chinese and the Siamese, like the British, were interested in them. Through negotiations with local rulers, the British were allowed to send resident advisers into the states.

Colonial Landmarks

Independence Square (*Dataran Merdeka*) is the center of the city of Kuala Lumpur and the site of several historic buildings dating from British colonial days. A huge flagpole on the green, which is claimed to be the world's tallest flagpole, was where the British flag was lowered when independence became official on August 31, 1957.

Across the street is a frequently photographed building that now houses the high courts of the nation. The Sultan Abdul Samad building (pictured), constructed in the 1890s, was the center of the colonial government. Instead of choosing a Malay style of architecture, the architects used elements of Indian, Moorish, and Arabic motifs. Arches, domes, pillars, and balustrades stretch down a long block. The governor of the Straits Settlements at the time considered the fanciful building a "ridiculous extravagance."

Other historic structures in the vicinity include the Moorish National History Museum and the Memorial Library, built in neo-Renaissance style. Adding to the mix is a red-roofed white mock-Tudor building, the Royal Selangor Club, and the neo-Gothic Anglican church, St. Mary's Cathedral. A few blocks away, towering over all the older buildings, are the two symbols of modern Malaysia's achievements, the KL Tower and the Petronas Twin Towers.

Throughout the rest of the nineteenth century, local rulers, British representatives, and Siam (now Thailand) jockeyed for power and influence in the Malay states. In 1896, four states—Selangor, Perak, Negeri Sembilan, and Pahang—became the Federated Malay States, with a capital at Kuala Lumpur. Gradually, Siam and Great Britain negotiated agreements that gave five non-Federated Malay states the status of British Protectorates. These five were Kelantan, Terengganu, Kedah, Perlis, and Johor. Thus twelve states on the peninsula (including the Straits Settlements) were under British rule by 1914.

Sarawak and Sabah

Sarawak, on the island of Borneo, is the largest state in Malaysia. Early in the nineteenth century, while the British were beginning to occupy and establish rule over the Straits Settlements, Sarawak was a small province headed by the sultan of Brunei. Unlike the people of the peninsula, who were mostly Malays, the people of Sarawak represented at least two dozen ethnic groups. Some of these early tribes had a reputation for being fierce and warlike. Pirates and headhunters roamed the rain forests and mountains of Borneo's interior.

The White Rajahs of Sarawak

In the early 1800s, a young English adventurer named James Brooke was visiting Kuching, Sarawak's major city. A local rajah, related to the sultan of Brunei, asked Brooke for assistance in suppressing a local uprising. The rebellion was put down, and Brooke persuaded the rajah that the people involved in it should be treated with compassion. Brooke won the respect of the people as well as of the rulers. In 1846, in an agreement with the sultan, Brooke agreed to assume the title of "rajah" and the job of ruling over Sarawak.

Brooke was the right man for the job. He was just and fair. He used local chieftains as advisers in settling disputes. He confronted pirates and headhunters, expanded the boundaries of the province, and brought law and order to the country. He ruled the area well until he died in 1868.

James Brooke meeting with a local ruler in 1842

Charles Brooke, who succeeded his uncle as rajah, concentrated on developing the region economically. His son, the third white rajah of Sarawak, carried on the traditions of respect for and cooperation with the native people. The three generations of the Brooke family governed Sarawak until 1941.

The Ranee of Sarawak

Margaret Brooke, wife of the second white rajah of Sarawak and mother of the third one, was a young English bride when she sailed to the far-off island of Borneo in the early 1870s. Until then, Margaret had lived the typical comfortable and sheltered life of a young English lady. She had learned several European languages and had some lessons in music and dancing but was totally unprepared for life in an undeveloped tropical Asian land.

Many years later, Margaret wrote a book about her experiences, *My Life in Sarawak*. Her descriptions of the climate, nature, foods, and native customs take readers to a place far away and long ago. She made close friends among the Malay and Dayak women of Sarawak, helped them when they were ill or in danger, and listened eagerly to their stories and confidences.

Margaret Brooke's curiosity and respect for the culture and people of Sarawak enriched her life and that of her readers as well. As she wrote, "I wanted to know about the country, and asked questions, but . . . I was gently made to understand that I had better find things out for myself."

Malaysian soldiers on patrol in World War II

Like Sarawak, Sabah was a land of diverse ethnic groups who lived in small communities ruled by chieftains. The sultans of Brunei and Sulu held loose control over the groups. From 1881 until 1946, the British-owned Chartered Company of North Borneo governed Sabah. However, during World War II, Japanese military forces occupied many of the coastal regions.

World War II

Japanese military forces invaded the Malay Peninsula in 1941. From there they attacked Singapore and forced Britain to give up its hold on the island. Britain lost all control over that part of the world until the end of the war, in 1945.

After the war, Singapore, Sarawak, and North Borneo (Sabah) became British colonies. The British formed the Malayan Union in 1946, which was replaced two years later by the Federation of Malaya. After several years of unrest and guerrilla fighting, the federation gained its independence from Britain in 1957.

A coalition of political parties known as Barisan Nasional has held majority control of the parliament ever since independence, except for a brief period between 1969 and 1971. In September 1963, Sarawak, Sabah, and Singapore united with Malaya to form a nation with a new name, Malaysia. Two years later, Singapore left Malaysia to become an independent nation in its own right.

Independence ceremony in 1957

Malaysia

Malays represented nearly half of the total population of the new nation. The Chinese were the second-largest ethnic group in numbers, but they had control over most of Malaysia's wealth. Indians made up the third most populous group. Racial tensions and resentments among the groups threatened the stability of the emerging government.

Malaysian police with
Indonesian prisoners in 1965

Periods of conflict marked the first few years of Malaysia's new union. Between 1963 and 1968 skirmishes broke out with Indonesia. These conflicts ended when a new chief executive took power in Indonesia. The Philippines, which had wanted to take over the state of Sabah, dropped its claim in 1968 and formally recognized Malaysia.

Malaysia's first prime minister, Tunku Abdul Rahman, was in power in 1969, when racial riots broke out, mainly in Kuala Lumpur. Hundreds of people were killed. As a result, the government declared a state of emergency and suspended the constitution. In 1970, the government announced the New Economic Policy. Its goal was to increase the share of the economy held by Malays. Racial quotas, scholarships, subsidies, and special economic schemes were introduced to help Malays.

Abdul Razak was elected prime minister in 1970. Parliamentary law was reinstated the following year. Razak served until his death, in 1976,

States of Malaysia

1 Federal Territory	5 Melaka	9 Perlis	13 Selangor
2 Johor	6 Negeri Sembilan	10 Pulau Pinang	14 Terengganu
3 Kedah	7 Pahang	11 Sabah	
4 Kelantan	8 Perak	12 Sarawak	

and he was followed by Hussein Onn. Mahathir bin Mohamad became the nation's fourth prime minister in 1981 and has held that office ever since.

The Mahathir Period

Prime Minister Mahathir bin Mohamad has been a strong leader who has encouraged economic development. Malaysia enjoyed a long period of expansion and prosperity in the 1980s. The nation has achieved international recognition for its achievements in manufacturing and construction. In 1996, the tallest building in the world, the Petronas Twin Towers, rose above Kuala Lumpur's skyline. It demonstrates to the whole world how rapidly Malaysia is advancing toward achieving its goals.

Prime Minister Mahathir bin Mohamad

Countries in eastern Asia began to suffer a serious downturn in their economies in 1997. Malaysian currency declined in value by 40 percent against the U.S. dollar. The financial crisis led to political unrest. Ibrahim Anwar, the deputy prime minister, supported a program of austerity and openly criticized Mahathir's handling of the crisis.

Mahathir did not agree. In 1998 he abruptly dismissed Anwar from the government and ordered his arrest. The following year, Mahathir dissolved the parliament and announced new elections. In spite of growing dissatisfaction with his dictatorial actions, Mahathir won the reelection.

Governing a Young Country

THE NATION OF MALAYSIA HAS A UNIQUE FORM OF GOVernment. It is similar to other countries in many ways, but very different in others. It is a federation of thirteen states, governed by a constitutional monarchy. After a long history as a colony of Great Britain, interrupted by a period of occupation by Japan during World War II, the Federation of Malaya was established as an independent nation in 1957.

In preparation for independence, a commission was assembled to write a constitution. Experts from the United Kingdom, Australia, India, and Pakistan participated in the project. In 1963, Singapore, Sabah, and Sarawak merged with Malaya to form Malaysia (Singapore later withdrew). Malaysia operates under the constitution of 1957, although many amendments have been added over the years.

The constitution declares that Bahasa Malaysia is the national language and must be used for official purposes. It also stipulates that no one may be prohibited or prevented from using or teaching any other language, except for official purposes.

Opposite: **Parliament buildings**

The Monarchy

Nine of the Malaysian states are governed by sultans. These sultans form the Conference of Rulers. Every five years, the conference meets to elect one of its members to serve as king of Malaysia—the Yang di-Pertuan Agong—for a

His Majesty

In December 2001, Tuanku Syed Sirajuddin was sworn in as Malaysia's new king. He was chosen by secret ballot by a vote of his peers.

five-year term. He resigns his position as a state ruler during his term as king but continues to be his state's religious leader.

The Yang di-Pertuan Agong is the head of state with certain discretionary powers, but most of his acts take effect on the advice of the cabinet and the prime minister. Malaysia has three branches of government at the federal level: executive, legislative, and judicial.

Citizenship and Elections

People can become Malaysian citizens in one of three ways: by registration, by naturalization, or by the incorporation of a territory where they reside. Registration includes those born in Malaysia and the children or spouses of Malaysian citizens. Foreign-born, non-Malaysian persons may become naturalized citizens if they meet certain requirements. Citizens of territories added to Malaysia, as Sabah and Sarawak were in 1963, are automatically given Malaysian citizenship.

All adult citizens have the right to vote. Elections are conducted by an elections commission, which is appointed by the Yang di-Pertuan Agong after consultation with the Conference of Rulers. Elections to the house of representatives, the *Dewan Rakyat*, are held every five years.

A coalition of political parties called Barisan Nasional has held national power in Malaysia through nine elections since the country's independence.

Casting a vote

Rukunegara

Rukunegara, a statement of five principles, outlines the Malaysian philosophy and outlook. The statement is an attempt to set forth universal concepts that all citizens can accept regardless of their ethnic origin or religious affiliation.

"Our nation, Malaysia, is dedicated to achieving a greater unity for all her peoples; to maintaining a democratic way of life; to creating a just society in which the wealth of the nation shall be equitably distributed; to ensuring a liberal approach to her rich and diverse cultural traditions; to building a progressive society which shall be orientated to modern science and technology.

"We, her peoples, pledge our united efforts to attain these ends guided by these principles:

1. Belief in God
2. Loyalty to King and Country
3. Supremacy of the Constitution
4. Rule of Law
5. Mutual Respect and Good Social Behavior"

The office of the prime minister in Putrajaya

The Executive Branch

In Malaysia, the executive branch of government is headed by the prime minister. After legislative elections, the head of the party that has won the greatest number of the seats in the house of representatives becomes the prime minister.

The cabinet is a council of ministers chosen from the membership of the house of representatives. Cabinet members are appointed by the king, with the advice of the prime minister. Each cabinet member administers one or more of the departments, or ministries, within the executive branch.

The administrative capital of Malaysia is now located in a new, modern, and beautifully planned city called Putrajaya. It is located about 14 miles (23 km) from Kuala Lumpur. Government office spaces were constructed within six years after the project was voted upon.

Well equipped with state-of-the-art communication and transportation facilities, Putrajaya is also a city of parks and gardens. About 70 percent of the total area is designed to remain green—lakes, wetlands, and landscaped regions surround large, attractive buildings. The Islam house of worship, Putra Mosque, occupies a prominent site. It is large enough to accommodate 15,000 worshipers at one time. Residential neighborhoods are also being developed.

The Prime Minister

Mahathir bin Mohamad became Malaysia's fourth prime minister in 1981. Dr. Mahathir was the first commoner to serve as head of the federation's executive branch—his predecessors had all been members of royal families. He was born in 1925, in the state of Kedah. He was educated as a doctor in Singapore and practiced medicine on Langkawi Island for a few years.

Dr. Mahathir had been active in politics since his student days, and in 1967 he was elected to Parliament. He lost his seat in the next election but won it back in 1974. Over the next few years, he held several posts in the administration.

In 1981 the political party known as UMNO (United Malays National Organization) chose Dr. Mahathir to be its president. That same year, he led his party to the first of five overwhelming victories in national elections. By 1999, Dr. Mahathir had been in power longer than any other elected leader in Asia.

Dr. Mahathir has been criticized for concentrating increasing power in the executive branch of Malaysia's government and for harshly squashing opposition to his rule. His tight control over the government, as well as his emphasis on developing the economy and building a widespread sense of pride in the nation's accomplishments, has helped him stay in office for more than twenty years.

National Ceremonial Symbols

Malaysia's national flag is called *Jalur Gemilang*, which means "a glorious range of values." It has fourteen alternating red and white stripes of equal width, with a dark blue rectangular field in the upper left corner. Within the blue field are a yellow crescent and

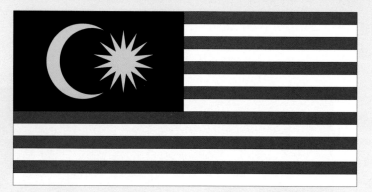

a fourteen-pointed star. The number fourteen stands for the thirteen states of the federation plus the federal government, all with equal status. The blue field stands for unity of the peoples of Malaysia. The star and crescent are the symbol of Islam, Malaysia's national religion. Yellow is the color of Malaysian royalty.

The star and crescent of Islam are in the center at the top of Malaysia's coat of arms. Below them is a shield, flanked by two tigers standing rampant. Symbols within the shield include five *keris* (daggers), symbols of the former unfederated Malay states of Johor, Kedah, Kelantan, Perlis, and Terengganu. Four panels in the center stand for the four former Federated Malay States of Negeri Sembilan, Pahang, Perak, and Selangor, in

the official colors of each state. Four other panels represent the states of Pulau Pinang and Sabah on the left, and Sarawak and Melaka on the right. The image of a hibiscus, the national flower, is in a panel in the center. A yellow ribbon beneath the shield bears the national motto, *Beresekutu Berbamtah Mutu* ("Unity Is Strength").

A yellow flag bearing the coat of arms is flown when the king is present.

The hibiscus, *bunga raya* in Malaysian, is the national flower. It was introduced to Malaysia by travelers, probably before the twelfth century. It grows abundantly in Malaysia in several colors and varieties. The official national flower is red, with five petals.

The keris ("kris" in English), a traditional Malaysian dagger, is a sacred weapon and a symbol of Malaysian history and culture. For many centuries, it was carried by every adult male and handed down from father to son. Today it is used for ceremonial purposes rather than combat. The Keris Panjang Di Raja is carried only by the Yang di-Pertuan Agong. It is gold-plated and bears the crest of the government and the eleven peninsular states in its hilt. It symbolizes the authority, royalty, and power of the king.

The orangutan, or "man of the forest," was used as an official mascot for the Commonwealth Games held in Malaysia in 1998. Intended to personify Malaysians as warm, friendly, and fun, the image of the orangutan is used to promote Malaysia's image all over the world.

National Symbols of Achievement

The Malaysian government recognizes certain recent national accomplishments as symbols of achievement, equal in importance to the more traditional ceremonial symbols.

Malaysia's National Monument (below) occupies a large area on top of a hill in the Lake Gardens in Kuala Lumpur. Besides the monument itself, the area includes a reflecting pool with fountain, a crescent-shaped pavilion, a cenotaph (memorial tomb), and gardens. The monument has seven bronze figures on an oblong base, representing different branches of Malaysian security forces. It is dedicated to those who have died in the cause of peace and freedom and symbolizes the triumph of the forces of democracy over the forces of evil. It was designed by an American sculptor, Felix de Weldon, who also created the famous Iwo Jima Memorial in Washington, D.C.

Parliament House is the symbol of democracy in Malaysia. Standing on a hill in the Lake Gardens, it is used for parliamentary sessions, offices, and special events.

Malaysia's automobile, the Proton Saga, may seem like an unusual national symbol, but Malaysians take great pride in this achievement. First produced in 1985, the Proton Saga signifies the determination of the nation to take its place in the international community of industrialized nations.

Menara Kuala Lumpur, a telecommunications tower (above), is a significant landmark and a tourist destination. An observation tower offers a panoramic view of Kuala Lumpur. Designed to meet the growing need for state-of-the-art technology, it has been hailed as "the symbol of a country that will stop at nothing less than excellence." The tallest tower in Asia, it was opened to the public in 1996.

Petronas Twin Towers are a stunning pair of connected towers that hold the title of tallest building in the world. Completed in 1996, the structure became recognized overnight as a world landmark and a national monument.

The Legislature

Malaysia's legislative body is a bicameral parliament. The two houses are a 69-member senate, *Dewan Negara*, and a 180-member house of representatives, Dewan Rakyat. The senate has much less power than the house of representatives. Almost all legislation is initiated in the Dewan Rakyat.

Members of the house of representatives are chosen by popular elections held every five years. Senators serve three-year terms. Most of the members of the senate—forty-three of them—are appointed by the king. The remaining twenty-six are selected by the state legislatures—two from each state. Rules of procedure in the Malaysian parliament are based on those of the British parliament.

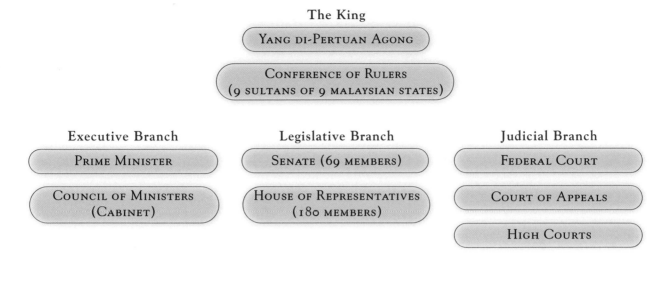

NATIONAL GOVERNMENT OF MALAYSIA

The King
YANG DI-PERTUAN AGONG

CONFERENCE OF RULERS
(9 SULTANS OF 9 MALAYSIAN STATES)

Executive Branch
PRIME MINISTER

COUNCIL OF MINISTERS
(CABINET)

Legislative Branch
SENATE (69 MEMBERS)

HOUSE OF REPRESENTATIVES
(180 MEMBERS)

Judicial Branch
FEDERAL COURT

COURT OF APPEALS

HIGH COURTS

The Judiciary

The constitution establishes three levels of courts in Malaysia: the federal court, the court of appeals, and the high courts. The federal court is the highest level. Judges are appointed by the Yang di-Pertuan Agong and are independent of the executive and legislative branches. They cannot be removed from office before retirement at 65, unless they are proved unfit for office. This autonomy is questionable, however. A number of judgments issued by the court indicate that the prime minister has a great deal of influence over the court.

Several other courts operate at the state level. Sessions courts have jurisdiction over criminal and civil matters. Magistrates courts try criminal and civil cases up to certain limits on the amount of liability and severity of sentences. Small claims courts deal with monetary disputes—claims are limited to RM (*ringgit*) 5,000. Juvenile courts hear cases where the offender is younger than 18. The special court tries cases brought either by or against the Yang di-Pertuan Agong.

State Administrations

The thirteen states of Malaysia are the pillars of the federation. Each state has its own ruler and is sovereign, with jurisdiction over all matters not specifically named in the constitution as belonging to the federal government. State governments follow the same general system as the federal government.

Goals of the Federal Government

Since 1970, the Malaysian government has outlined its goals and standards for development in a series of five-year plans. The overall goal is to become a fully developed nation in the eyes of the world by the year 2020. Economic development has a high priority. Unfortunately, economic goals are often in conflict with protection of the environment and the quality of life for individuals.

Malaysian National Anthem

My country, my native land
The people living united and progressive
May God bestow blessing and happiness
May our Ruler have a successful reign
May God bestow blessing and happiness
May our Ruler have a successful reign.

Kuala Lumpur: Did You Know This?

Kuala Lumpur is situated on the Klang River, about 25 miles (40 km) from the west coast of peninsular Malaysia. The city was settled in the 1800s and grew quickly during British rule. It is noted for its architecture—traditional Moorish buildings mixed with modern office structures.

Population: 1,145,342 (1991)

Year Founded: 1857

Altitude: 128 feet (39 m) above sea level

Average Daily Temperature: 81°F (27°C) January and July

Average Annual Rainfall: 96 inches (244 cm)

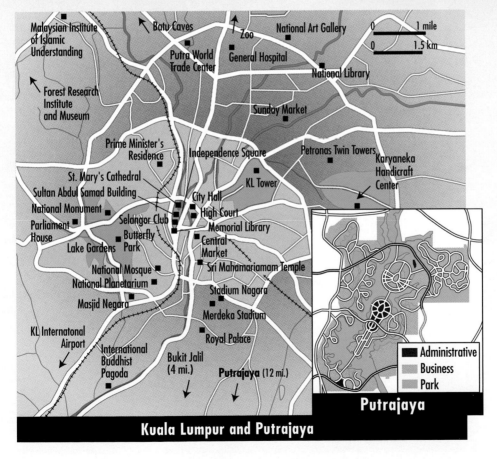

Kuala Lumpur and Putrajaya

Putrajaya

Administrative
Business
Park

Earning a Living

LONG BEFORE EUROPEAN EXPLORERS BEGAN TO TRAVEL across the Atlantic Ocean, traders from Persia, Arabia, and other parts of the world were sailing eastward across the Indian Ocean and the South China Sea. India, China, and various islands in the region were rich sources of silks, porcelains, jewels, and spices. Travelers making the journey between the ports of Calcutta, India, and Shanghai, China, found a good stopover at the southern end of the long strip of land now known as the Malay Peninsula. Before long, European adventurers—Portuguese, Dutch, and later English—joined the parade of merchants and traders to the region.

Most of the Malay people were not affected much by the activity in the peninsula's ports. They were, for the most part, people who made their living from the fields, forests, and waterways of their abundant land.

Opposite: **Farming in West Malaysia**

Waterways are important to Malaysia's economy.

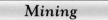

The history of mining in Malaysia begins long before modern times. The oldest known name of the region is *Aurea Chersonesus*, or "peninsula of gold." Some gold is still mined in both West and East Malaysia. But for a long time, first tin and then petroleum have been much more important mineral resources for the country.

In the middle of the nineteenth century, a new invention led to a major development on the Malay Peninsula. Searching for new ways to preserve and store foods, someone came up with the idea of shaping metal into a cylinder that could be sealed at both ends. We call this container a tin can. Today, it is usually made of other metals, but at first it was constructed of tin. Almost overnight, a worldwide demand for tin arose.

Tin ore had been mined on the Malay Peninsula for centuries, and this new market brought wealth to many local chiefs. Chinese and other investors opened mines, and new settlements sprang up around them. Kuala Lumpur, Malaysia's capital city, started as a small tin-mining settlement. There were not enough local workers to fill the demand for miners, so the mine owners imported laborers from India and China.

For many decades, Chinese investors had a nearly complete monopoly on tin mining. The Malay

Stacking tin ingots for shipment

An oil refinery

Peninsula supplied more than half of the world's supply of tin. Perak's Kinta Valley became the tin capital of the world.

The situation has changed drastically in recent years. World prices for tin have fluctuated so greatly that one of the world's largest tin mines, Sungai Lembing, closed and reopened several times during the past century. Many of Malaysia's tin mines have been completely closed up and filled in. Housing and commercial developments have been built over the old mines.

Petroleum has taken the place of tin in economic importance to Malaysia. Oil and natural gas fields exist in Sarawak and Sabah, as well as on the east coast of the Malay Peninsula and in offshore fields in the South China Sea.

Other mineral resources in Malaysia include iron ore, gold, antimony, bauxite, and small quantities of gemstones in Sarawak.

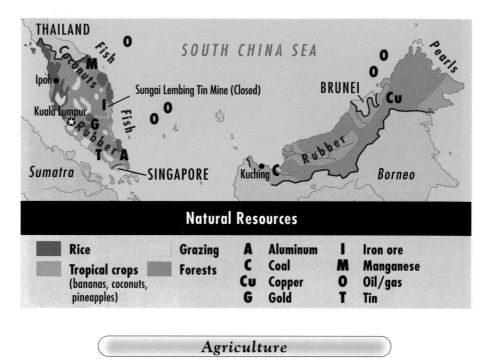

THAILAND

SOUTH CHINA SEA

Ipoh

Sungai Lembing Tin Mine (Closed)

Kuala Lumpur

BRUNEI

Sumatra

SINGAPORE

Kuching

Borneo

Pearls

Natural Resources

▮ Rice	▮ Grazing	**A**	Aluminum	**I**	Iron ore
▮ Tropical crops	▮ Forests	**C**	Coal	**M**	Manganese
(bananas, coconuts,		**Cu**	Copper	**O**	Oil/gas
pineapples)		**G**	Gold	**T**	Tin

Agriculture

Malaysia has an abundance of natural resources. The products of its fields, forests, and mines have been the foundation of its economy. Most of the Malay people have made a living from farming and fishing.

Until recently, nearly two-thirds of the country's population lived in rural areas. Not long ago, there had been a big rush from the countryside to the city. The nation's leadership wants to see the country move quickly toward complete industrialization, and this will result in higher migration from rural regions to urban areas.

From its earliest days of trading with other nations, Malaysia has grown crops for export. Sugarcane, bananas, pepper, and coconuts were some of these products. Some of the leading export crops today are pineapples, coconuts, tea, coffee, and cassavas. Much of the world's supply of black pepper comes from Sarawak. Rice is the nation's most important food crop, but today Malaysia has to import some rice from Thailand and Myanmar to feed its own population.

For a number of years, the Malaysian government tried to encourage small farming by offering aid as an incentive for people to raise crops. In the 1990s this policy was reversed, because small farming did not always prove practical. Farmers found that they could not earn enough income on the small farms, and many of them migrated to cities in search of jobs with greater security and better pay. The government turned its support to large-scale farming.

Sorting tea leaves

Rubber and Palm Oil

Just as the invention of the tin can brought a mining boom to the Malay Peninsula, the beginning of the automobile age and the invention of automobile tires ushered in a rubber boom. Rubber trees are not native to Malaysia—they came originally from Brazil. But by the end of the nineteenth century, rubber plantations covered about 7,500 square miles (19,425 sq km) of the peninsula. Malaysia became the world's leading producer of crude rubber.

Harvesting Rubber

Workers on rubber plantations are called tappers. They go out early in the morning to "tap" the trees. They cut grooves in the bark of a tree with sharp knives, insert metal spouts at the point of the grooves, and hang cups from the spouts. A milky substance called latex drips into the cup. The cups are emptied later in the day, and the latex is processed into crude rubber.

Rubber created great wealth for this small Asian country. Between 1900 and 1940, one of the most stable economies in the entire region was on the Malay Peninsula, due mainly to products of the rubber tree.

What Malaysia Grows, Makes, and Mines	
Agriculture (1996)	
Palm oil	8,386,000 metric tons
Rice	2,065,000 metric tons
Sugarcane	1,600,000 metric tons
Manufacturing (1995)	
Cement	10,713,000 metric tons
Refined sugar	1,052,000 metric tons
Fertilizer	269,000 metric tons
Mining	
Iron ore (1996)	325,114 metric tons
Bauxite (1996)	218,680 metric tons
Coal (1994)	174,000 metric tons
Crude petroleum (1994)	237,742,000 barrels
Natural gas (1994)	24,411,000,000 cubic meters

In the 1950s, palm oil began to replace rubber as Malaysia's most important agricultural product. Many rubber plantations changed to the cultivation of oil palms. Nearly 2 million acres (809,371 hectares) are now covered with palms, and Malaysia produces more than half of the world output of palm oil.

Genetic research at a palm-oil plantation

Timber

Malaysia's forests have been a major source of employment, and timber is an important commodity for export. Unfortunately, the valuable old trees are being cut down at a much faster rate than they can be replaced. The new trees that are planted grow faster and do not develop as dense a root structure as the older ones had. This can create serious erosion of the soil. In the space of only a few years, the irreplaceable rain forests could disappear, replaced only partially with tree plantations.

Sarawak has the largest acreage of forests of all the Malaysia states. Even in the early years of international trade, the people of East Malaysia gathered jungle products for export. A number of the residents of the river town of Sibu in Sarawak have become quite wealthy through the timber trade.

Measuring commercial logs

Conserving the Rain Forests

Conservation activists within Malaysia and in the international community are deeply concerned about the loss of the rain forests and the environmental consequences. The "greenhouse effect" can cause irreversible changes in the climate across most of the globe. Some species of animal life may become extinct as their habitat is destroyed. Researchers depend heavily on the study of forest plants in search of new drugs.

In an attempt to slow down the destruction of rain forests, the Malaysian government is making an effort to discourage the shipment of rough logs to foreign nations. The Malaysian economy could profit in the long run by cutting fewer trees and using the logs at home to manufacture wood products.

Manufacturing

Malaysia's economic wealth has up to now depended on its natural resources. The mining, agriculture, and forestry sectors have provided jobs and revenue. But these sectors are declining, and the economic future of the country lies in finding alternative sources of income. Malaysia hopes to become a thoroughly modern, industrialized country within the next few years. A major part of the plan is to increase processing of the nation's raw materials into finished goods. Furniture, veneers, and plywood are a few of the goods made from forest products. Rubber goods for domestic use as well as for export can be manufactured from the nation's rich supply of latex. Chemicals and plastics are byproducts of petroleum.

Only about one-fourth of the labor force of Malaysia is employed in manufacturing, but the industry's importance is increasing. In 1991, manufactured goods made up 65 percent of Malaysia's exports to other countries. By 1999, this share had increased to more than 85 percent. Electronics, electrical machinery, and appliances were the most important

System of Weights and Measures

The standard system of weights and measures is the metric system. For example, 1 kilometer equals 0.6 miles; 1 kilogram equals 2.2 pounds. However, British imperial units are still used also. For example, 1 litre equals 0.26 U.S. gallons but 0.22 imperial gallons.

Money Facts

The basic unit of currency in Malaysia is the ringgit (RM). Each ringgit is made up of 100 *sen*, or cents. Paper currency comes in denominations of RM2, RM5, RM10, RM20, RM50, RM100, RM500, and RM1000. Coins are 1, 5, 10, 20, and 50 sen, and RM1.

A picture of the first elected king of Malaysia, Tuanku Abdul Rahman, wearing the royal head-dress and uniform, is on the face of all bills. The national flower, the hibiscus, also appears on all bills.

The RM1 note depicts East Malaysia, with a coastal scene and a picture of Gunung Kinabalu, the highest mountain in Southeast Asia. The other notes illustrate industrial accomplishments of Malaysia. The Kuala Lumpur tele-communications tower and a satellite launched by Malaysia are pictured on the RM2 bill. The Petronas Twin Towers and images from the Kuala Lumpur International Airport appear on the RM5 note. Transportation is represented on the RM10 note by a train, a ship, and an airplane. Pictures on the RM50 note illustrate the oil industry, a very important segment of the Malaysian economy. An assembly line of Proton Sagas, Malaysia's national car, is portrayed on the RM100 note.

Malaysian coins are decorated with images of several Malaysian artifacts: the keris, the *gungaraya* (kite), and a drum. The National Parliament building and the Islamic star and crescent are pictured on the 50-sen and 10-sen coins.

manufactured products exported—about 70 percent of the total. By the turn of the century, Malaysia had become the largest exporter of semiconductor components to the United States.

Foreign investors, especially the Japanese, have helped to promote manufacturing in Malaysia. Mitsubishi, a Japanese

Working on a Proton Saga assembly line

firm, helped Malaysians to manufacture the first automobile made and designed in Southeast Asia, the Proton Saga. This car is popular in several other Asian countries as well as in Malaysia. Malaysia also produces trucks and tractors.

Tourism

Tourism in Malaysia has grown in importance to the country's economy. The most important destinations are the beaches, where people can enjoy the tropical climate in luxurious resorts and hotels. In contrast, many tourists are also drawn to the unusual experiences available in East Malaysia. Jungle safaris with lodging in longhouses provide a look into a different side of this interesting country.

In Malaysia, tourism is one of the top three sources of foreign income. Domestic tourism—people traveling through their own country—is increasing.

High Tech

A strip of land 31 miles by 9 miles (50 km by 14 km) extending from the Petronas Twin Towers to the Kuala Lumpur International Airport is being developed according to an experimental, highly imaginative plan. Called the Multimedia Super Corridor (MSC), the project is intended to encourage and assist many international partners in exploring new ways of using the latest tools of information technology. The corridor is intended to become a high-tech research and development hub for international communications. It is hoped that by the year 2020 Malaysia's developmental goals and objectives will have been met.

Universiti Putra Malaysia, established in 1969, is becoming a supertechnology campus. It will play an important role in the MSC, along with research institutions, technology parks, industrial zones, and the new administrative capital city of Putrajaya.

Transportation

Historically, transportation by water has provided the major means of transportation through Malaysia. The long coastline of the peninsula has made sea travel essential. In the dense inland regions of East Malaysia, rivers have been the main arteries of transit. River transport is still important in Sabah and Sarawak, but peninsular Malaysia has one of the best road networks in that part of the world. High-quality roads and rail networks have linked all but the most remote parts of the peninsula. A railroad from Singapore to Bangkok, Thailand, connects all the major cities in West Malaysia.

Airline service is growing rapidly in Malaysia. International airports are Johor Bahru, Kuala Lumpur, and Pulau Pinang. In addition, a fleet of small aircraft provides services to remote areas of East Malaysia.

Train at a subway station in Kuala Lumpur

Planning

The Malaysian government takes a strong leadership role in the nation's economy. Economists credit the rapid growth in the 1980s and early 1990s to the mixed economy—a combination of private enterprise, state corporations, and foreign investment.

One Nation, Many Peoples

74

MOST MALAYSIANS ARE OF MALAY, CHINESE, OR Indian descent. But there are also many groups of native people whose ancestors have lived here for hundreds or maybe thousands of years.

When merchant ships began sailing into harbors along the coast of the Malay Peninsula long ago, they met people who lived in small settlements along the coast and in the interior. The newcomers, mostly traders from China and India in the early days, brought goods. They also brought their own customs and beliefs. Some of them stayed on the peninsula and established businesses and homes there.

In the eighteenth and nineteenth centuries, the need for workers in the mines and plantations of the Malay Peninsula brought additional waves of immigration from other Asian countries.

Opposite: **Traditional dancers perform in Sabah.**

Who Lives in Malaysia? (1997)		
Ethnic group	Number	Percentage of population
Malay	10,254,000	51
Other bumiputra	2,178,000	11
Chinese	5,430,000	27
Indian	1,538,000	8
Others	678,000	3
Total	20,078,000	100

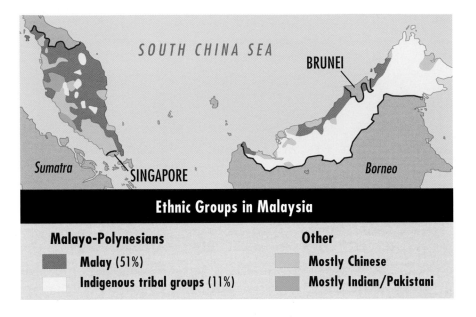

Ethnic Groups in Malaysia

Malayo-Polynesians
- Malay (51%)
- Indigenous tribal groups (11%)

Other
- Mostly Chinese
- Mostly Indian/Pakistani

Young Malaysians

Today's Malaysians are descended from this mixture of people. There are two major divisions in the society—the *bumiputra* and the *non-bumiputra*. Bumiputra means "sons of the soil." It is the name given to those whose cultures are native to the region. These include the *Orang Asli* and Malays of peninsular Malaysia, as well as the indigenous tribal people of Sarawak and Sabah. The largest groups of nonbumiputras are people of Chinese, Indian, Peranakan, and Eurasian descent.

When the nation of Malaysia was created, its leaders faced some difficult problems. The overall challenge was to build a new, united nation of millions of people who speak dozens of mother tongues, follow many religions, and have vastly different traditions. Malays make up a little more than half of the total population. However, most Malays are poorer, more likely to live in rural areas, and less educated than some other citizens, especially the Chinese. Malays owned only 2 percent of the nation's corporate wealth in 1963. Nearly all the top jobs in business and finance were held by the Chinese.

A rural family outside their home

Malays were determined to correct these inequalities. They were especially afraid of the dominance the Chinese held in Singapore. So in 1965, it was decided that Singapore should be a separate nation from Malaysia.

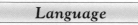
Bahasa Malaysia is the official language of Malaysia. It is related to many other languages of the South Pacific. A standardized combination of Malay dialects, it is much like Bahasa Indonesia, the language of the country south of Malaysia. Speakers of either language can understand much of what is said in the other one.

Dozens of languages have been used to conduct business in the Malay Peninsula over the centuries, because it has been

A multilingual shop sign

Bahasa Malaysia

Bahasa Malaysia's grammar is simple in structure. There are no articles, tenses, or genders. To form the plural of a word, one simply says it twice. Pronunciation is easy, for the most part. Here is how to pronounce the vowels:

a as in father
e as in pet
i as in pit
o as in hop
u as in put

As for consonants, the sound "ch" is spelled simply "c," and "sh" is spelled "sy." Other consonants sound as they usually do in English.

Here are a few everyday phrases in Bahasa Malaysia:

Selamat pagi	Good morning (literally, "peaceful morning")
Abat khabar?	What's new?
Selamat tinggal	Goodbye
Nama saya Mary.	My name is Mary.
Bolehkah tolong saya?	Can you help me?
Terima kasih	Thank you
Sama-sama	You're welcome
Saya suka berada di sini.	I like it here.
Maafkan saya.	Excuse me.
Tidak	No

such an important crossroads of commerce. As a result, many words borrowed from other languages—including Arabic, Chinese, Sanskrit, Persian, Portuguese, Dutch, and English—have crept into common use in Malaysia.

Not every Malaysian speaks the official language. People in Sarawak and Sabah use it infrequently, preferring to speak the traditional language of their own ethnic groups. Many Malaysians learn English, and it is widely spoken, especially in the cities and in business and technology. Most urban Chinese and Indians know and use English as well as their own languages. People also pick up a lot of English from television programs coming from the United States, Britain, and Australia. A mixture of Bahasa Malaysia and English has developed, popularly called Manglish.

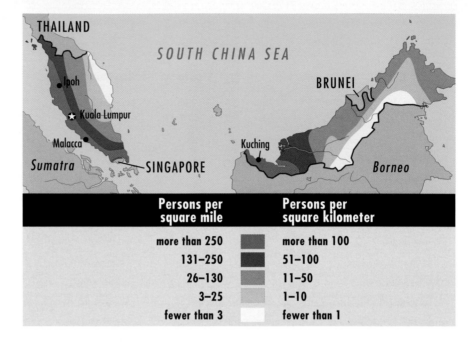

Persons per square mile		Persons per square kilometer
more than 250		more than 100
131–250		51–100
26–130		11–50
3–25		1–10
fewer than 3		fewer than 1

Population of Major Cities (1991)

Kuala Lumpur	1,145,342
Ipoh	382,853
Johor Baharu	328,436
Melaka	296,897
Petaling Jaya	254,350

Population of Malaysian States (1999)

*Johor	2,513,000
*Kedah	1,579,000
*Kelantan	1,446,000
Melaka	609,000
*Negeri Sembilan	820,000
*Pahang	1,251,000
*Perak	2,229,000
*Perlis	217,000
Pulau Pinang	1,253,000
Sabah	2,197,000
Sarawak	2,000,000
*Selangor	2,848,000
*Terenggan	957,000
Federal Territory	1,410,000
TOTAL	**21,329,000**

*Governed by sultans, who are members of the Conference of Rulers.

Population Distribution

The latest census for Malaysia showed a total population of 21,329,000. With a total area of 127,310 square miles (329,733 sq km), the population density was about 158 people per square mile (51 per sq km). This is a lower ratio than most of the nation's neighbors. As of 1980, a little less than two-thirds of Malaysians lived in rural areas. Since then, many people have left the rural areas for towns and cities, particularly in West Malaysia.

Orang Asli

Orang Asli means "original people," and it refers to descendants of various groups

who inhabited the peninsula before the Malays came. The oldest of these groups, the Smang, lived a nomadic life as hunters and gatherers in the mountainous interior of the peninsula.

The Senoi are thought to have migrated from the hill regions of Kampuchea and Vietnam between 6,000 and 8,000 years ago. A third group, the Proto-Malays, closely related to modern Malays, arrived later. Both the Senoi and the Proto-Malays were traditionally hunters, farmers, and fishers.

Malays

Malays make up a little more than half of the population of Malaysia. Their history in Southeast Asia and the surrounding seas goes back at least 3,000 years. Malays of the peninsula were related to others who lived across the Straits of Malacca. They traveled back and forth across the straits easily and often.

Malays were traditionally farmers who lived a simple life in a kampung (village). The majority still live in rural areas working in rice fields, on rubber plantations, or as fishers. Some, however, have moved to the cities, lured by jobs in business and government.

Muslim women in the city

Malaysian law states that its citizens have freedom of religion. On the other hand, Islam is the official national religion, and it is mandated by law that only followers of Islam can be classified as Malays.

Chinese

More than one-fourth of Malaysia's population is Chinese. The Chinese began to migrate to the region several hundred years ago. The largest numbers, however, came during the nineteenth century. They worked very hard, often at difficult jobs such as heavy construction. They played a large part in the development of the tin industry.

The Chinese for the most part held onto their own traditions and culture rather than integrating into Malay society. Their close ties with family and clans and their history as traders helped them to succeed in business. By the end of the nineteenth century, the Chinese owned most of the businesses on the peninsula.

Today's Chinese Malaysians are mostly businesspeople and shopkeepers and live in towns and cities. They speak several dialects; the most commonly used is Cantonese.

A Chinese shopkeeper

An Indian student from Penang

Indians

The third-largest ethnic group in Malaysia is Indians. They make up about 8 percent of the total population. Early Indian traders had a significant influence on Malaysian history, culture, and language. Unlike the Chinese, however, few of them made permanent homes in this country.

During British colonial times, Indian laborers were imported in large numbers to work on plantations. They came because they received better pay than they could earn at home. Most of the descendants, along with later immigrants, speak Tamil. Some of them live in the larger towns on the west coast of peninsular Malaysia, and besides agriculture they are involved in a variety of occupations, such as commerce, finance, and services. However, quite a few people of Indian descent are still employed as plantation workers and live at poverty level.

Peranakans

The Peranakan culture grew out of mixed marriages between upper-class Chinese merchants and local Malay women beginning in the thirteenth century. Peranakan is a Malay word meaning "born here." The descendants of these early marriages added more and more Chinese immigrants to the mixture and came to be known as Straits Chinese.

It is said that the Peranakan cuisine, dress, and customs combine the best of both heritages. The culture reached its height during the late nineteenth century, mostly in Melaka, Pulau Pinang, and Singapore.

Eurasians

After the Portuguese invaded Melaka in 1511, the European soldiers were encouraged to marry local women and raise Catholic families. Even 500 years later, some communities include many people who have Portuguese names and still honor some traditions of their ancestors. A few other Malaysians, equally proud of their heritage, trace their ancestry to intermarriage between locals and Dutch or English ancestors.

People of Sabah

The province of Sabah, on the northeastern corner of East Malaysia, is the most diverse of all the sections of this very diversified country. People have lived in remote, scattered communities along the coast and in the forests and jungles of Borneo's mountainous interior for thousands of years. Most of today's inhabitants are believed to be descendants of Mongoloid settlers who reached the island some 5,000 years ago.

Muslim Names

Malay people, as well as Muslim Indians, do not use surnames. A person has a given name, followed by *bin* ("son of") or *binte* ("daughter of"), then the father's name—for example, Ahmad bin Abdullah (Ahmad, son of Abdullah), or Fatima binte Omar (Fatima, daughter of Omar). One should never call a person by the second name.

Within a family, people rarely use given names. They call each other by their position in the family, such as "youngest niece" or "oldest uncle."

This Dusun tribesman lives in Sabah.

The 2 million people of Sabah represent at least thirty ethnic groups, who speak countless dialects and languages. About 30 percent of the population belong to a group of somewhat related tribes, or clans, known as Kadazan/Dusuns. Most of them now practice Christianity along with some observance of older ceremonies and rituals. They cultivate rice farms and live on coastal plains and interior valleys.

A large group of people called Bajau migrated from the southern tip of the Malay Peninsula several centuries ago. Many live in houses perched on stilts along the water. They are fishers and farmers, and most of them are Muslims. Other colorful tribes live in the interior.

These ethnic groups are part of Malaysia's bumiputra. In addition, there are Chinese and Indonesian communities in Sabah.

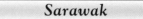

Sarawak

About half of the population of Sarawak are bumiputra. As in Sabah, these people comprise several dozen distinct ethnic groups. In addition, more than 20 percent of the population are Malays; slightly more than that are Chinese.

Native ethnic groups in Sarawak are divided into four sectors. The largest are the Iban, or Sea Dyaks, followed by

Bidayuh (Land Dayaks), Melanau, and a group of seventeen or more tribes known collectively as the Orang Ulu.

The Iban are descendants of warriors once known as head-hunters. During the nineteenth century they controlled the rivers, traveling by canoe and depending largely on fishing for a living. These were the people whose rebellion against the sultan's rule in the nineteenth century resulted in the establishment of James Brooke as a white rajah.

The majority of Sarawak's indigenous people now live in developed towns and cities, but some still follow old ways. Colorful festivals keep old traditions alive.

Some Dayaks still follow traditional ways.

Faiths to Follow

ANCIENT PEOPLE IN MALAYSIA, AS IN MOST OF THE world, were animists. They believed that different spirits exist in forces of nature. Some people who follow the major religions of today still retain a few rituals and practices that have been handed down from these ancient beliefs.

Religion plays an important part in Malaysian culture and everyday life. Religion is closely tied to ethnicity in this multiethnic country. For example, almost without exception, Malays are Muslim. In fact, only followers of Islam can legally claim to be ethnic Malays. Most Indian-Malaysians are either Hindus or Sikhs. The majority of Chinese-Malaysians are followers of Confucianism, Taoism, Buddhism, or traditional Chinese ancestor worship. Christianity crosses ethnic lines to a large extent, as does the Baha'i faith.

Opposite: **Kedah State Mosque**

Buddhists praying at a temple

Islam is the official religion of Malaysia, but the constitution guarantees freedom of religion for everyone. It states that each religious group has the right to manage its own affairs and that no one can be compelled to pay taxes to support religious institutions. Religious groups are free to make efforts to recruit members, except that non-Muslims are prohibited from making efforts to convert Muslims.

Religion and Government

Malaysia is not an Islamic state, because it is not governed by Islamic law. However, Islam does have the full encouragement, including financial backing, of the federal government. At the state level, there is a closer link between religion and government. Nine of the eleven states of West Malaysia are governed by sultans, who are hereditary rulers. These sultans are the head of Islam, as well as of the government, in each of their states. The Yang di-Pertuan Agong (king of Malaysia) is the head of Islam for the other four states (Melaka, Pulau Pinang, Sarawak, and Sabah) and the Federal Territory. He also has the authority to determine dates for the observance of nationwide religious observances.

Muslim courts (*syariah*) have jurisdiction only over Muslims and only in the case of offenses against the principles of Islam.

Islam

A little more than half of the people of Malaysia are Muslims. Most of them are Malay, but some Indians, Chinese,

Kadazans, and a few other non-Malays are also followers of Islam. Arab traders introduced their faith to people of the Malay Peninsula in the thirteenth century or earlier. By that time, the religion was strong on the nearby island of Sumatra.

Melaka's first ruler became a convert to Islam in 1410, and over the following century that city became an important center of Islamic scholarship.

The religion is based on certain principles, called the Pillars of Islam. The first is *Shahada*, the belief that there is no god but Allah and that Mohammad is his messenger. *Salat* means "worship." Faithful Muslims face the holy city of Mecca and offer prayers. Friday midday prayers are especially important. *Zakat* means "charity." Muslims are expected to

Religions of Malaysia

Muslim	53%
Buddhist	17%
Chinese traditional religions	12%
Hindu	7%
Christian	6%
Other	5%

The National Mosque

Masjid Negara, the National Mosque, is the major Muslim center in Kuala Lumpur. Its modern design uses Islamic art and calligraphy in its decor. The Grand Hall, always very busy on Fridays, is large enough to hold 8,000 people at their prayers. It has a jagged eighteen-point blue roof that from the air looks like a partially open umbrella. The eighteen points stand for the five pillars of Islam and the thirteen states of Malaysia. A garden covering 13 acres (5 ha) is a burial ground for some of Malaysia's most important leaders. A minaret towers over the complex.

give 10 percent of their wealth, called a tithe, each year to help the poor. *Saum* means "fasting." During the holy month of Ramadan, Muslims are forbidden to eat, drink, or smoke during daylight hours. *Hadj* means "pilgrimage." All devout Muslims, if they can afford it, are supposed to make a trip to Mecca some time during their lives.

Buddhism

Buddhism is the second most widespread religious faith in Malaysia. Nearly a fifth of the nation's population practices one of the two major schools of Buddhist thought. Mahayana (Greater Path) Buddhism is the Chinese version. Theravada (Little Path) is followed by Malaysians of Thai and other Southeast Asian ancestry. Buddhists try to follow an Eightfold Path to Enlightenment, which consists of right understanding, right thought, right speech, right conduct, right livelihood, right effort, right attentiveness, and right concentration.

Chinese Buddhists are more numerous than the other ethnic groups in Malaysia. There are several thousand temples, societies, and organizations of Chinese Buddhists. All of these are autonomous, but most belong to the Malaysian Buddhist Association. Chinese merchants introduced Buddhism to the Malay Peninsula centuries ago, but most of today's Chinese Buddhists are descended from the immigrants who arrived during the nineteenth and early twentieth centuries. Kwan Yin, the goddess of mercy, and Kwan Ti, the god of war, are important figures in Mahayana observances.

Thai Buddhists came to the peninsula during the eighteenth century. Their observances are simpler and more abstract than those of the Chinese.

A third and smaller Buddhist group in Malaysia follows the teachings of a thirteenth-century Japanese leader named Nichiren Daishonin. Nichiren Buddhists use chanting in their services. Activities are organized by lay groups, not monks. The emphasis is on activities to promote peace, culture, and education, based on Buddhism.

Statue of Kwan Yin, the Buddhist goddess of mercy

Other Chinese Religions

Confucianism and Taoism are deeply rooted in Chinese culture. Some people argue that these are philosophies or simply ways of life according to certain ethical principles rather than religions. However, along with a mixture of ideas, beliefs, and traditions of ancestor worship, they are often organized around a self-governing temple and are generally regarded as Chinese religions. About one-tenth of the Malaysian population practice Confucianism and Taoism.

Confucius

Confucius was a wise man who lived around 500 B.C. His family was poor, and his father died while he was an infant. His mother, however, made sure he got the best education possible. By the time he was 15, he was determined to be a scholar, and he taught others for more than fifty years.

The teachings of Confucius emphasized certain virtues. Among them were kindness and love for others, morality and duty to one's neighbors, and doing what is right rather than what will benefit oneself. Rulers, Confucious taught, should set a good example and not use force and violence. A government that teaches by example will influence citizens to control themselves. "Your job is to govern, not to kill," and "The way the wind blows, that's the way the grass bends " illustrate his advice to rulers. The underlying principle of ethics and morality according to Confucius is "What you do not like done to yourself, do not do unto others."

A Hindu Celebration

The Sri Mahamariamman Hindu Temple in Kuala Lumpur is a spectacular example of Indian sacred architecture. It is a tall, tapered structure covered with brilliantly colored figures of gods. Each January, the Hindu festival of Thaipusam draws a million or so spectators to watch a procession of worshipers proceed from this temple to the Batu Caves, just outside the city. The participants carry offerings of fruit and flowers and climb a difficult flight of 272 concrete steps that lead to the entrance of the limestone caves.

Rock climbers and fans of cave exploration visit the Batu Caves, too. The largest cavern is called Cathedral Cave. Colorful drawings of Hindu legends decorate the walls of another one of the caves.

Hinduism and Sikhism

Most Indian Malaysians today are Hindus. Traders from the Indian subcontinent brought their religion and their culture to the Malay Peninsula around the first century B.C. This early version of Hinduism was an aristocratic religion, popular with members of the ruling class, and later replaced by Islam.

For the most part, Indian immigrants of the nineteenth and early twentieth centuries brought their own Hindu practices and traditions. These vary to a great extent according to what part of India the immigrants came from. Hindu temples are run by local committees. Hindu youth groups are very active.

About one out of eight Indian Malaysians are Sikhs. Another sect that originated in India, Sikhism dates to the fifteenth century. Traditional Hinduism recognizes more than one god. This type of religion is called pantheism. The founder of Sikhism converted his followers to monotheism, a belief in one god. A Sikh house of worship is called a *Gurdwara* and is open to all people regardless of race, religion, color, or sex.

Christianity

The Portuguese who conquered Melaka in 1511 brought Christianity with them. They married local women, and their descendants were raised as Christians. Some of these descendants still live in the region. During British colonial days in the nineteenth century, Christian missionaries founded schools and hospitals in Malaysia and gained converts. Today about 1 million people, or about 6 percent of the national population, are members of Christian churches. The membership cuts across ethnic lines. Small numbers of Indians and Chinese belong to Christian churches on the peninsula. Larger groups are in Sabah and Sarawak, including Ibans, Bidayuhs, Kedayans, Kadazan/Dusuns, and Muruts. Christian denominations in Malaysia include Roman Catholics, Anglicans, Methodists, Presbyterians, and a number of smaller churches.

Malaysian Christians of Chinese, Eurasian, and Indian descent gather in Melaka on Good Friday and Easter Sunday. They take part in a candlelit procession to St. Peter's Church. St. Peter's was built by the Dutch in 1710.

St. Peter's Church in Melaka

Traditional Weddings

Wedding practices of Malaysia's ethnic communities are illustrated in a series of exhibits arranged around a large room in Kuala Lumpur's National Museum. Visitors can see the different kinds of elaborate costumes, traditions, and gifts that are characteristic of marriage ceremonies as celebrated by the different people of Malaysia's multicultural society.

Baha'i

The Baha'i religion has a small but worldwide membership. It was founded in Persia in 1844 and introduced to Malaysia in 1953. About 1 percent of Malaysia's population is Baha'i. They include Chinese, Indians, Ibans, Kadazans, and other non-Muslim bumiputras.

Baha'is teach that all great religions are essentially alike, that "all roads lead to the same God." Some of their fundamental goals include the elimination of prejudices, equality of the sexes, universal education, and establishment of a world federation.

Festivals

Festivals in Malaysia bring people together across religious and ethnic lines. Major religious holidays are also official national holidays. Members of all levels of society, including royalty and top political leaders, hold parties in their homes. People of all religions are welcomed to come together. Even tourists are often invited to join the festivities.

Many state or local holidays are celebrated in addition to those observed nationally. Dates of some of the holidays vary from year to year because they are based on calendars other than the one used internationally today.

Important Religious Holidays of Malaysia

Wesak Day	May
Deepavali	October or November
Christmas Day	December 25

The dates for the following Islamic holidays vary greatly from year to year.

Hari Raya Haji

Hari Raya Puasa

Muslim New Year

Prophet Muhammad's Birthday

Major Malaysian Festivals

The two most important Muslim holidays are Hari Raya Puasa and Hari Raya Haji. Hari Raya Puasa is held for two days at the end of the monthlong fasting season of Ramadan. People celebrate with visits, feasts, new clothes, and newly cleaned and decorated homes. It is also a time when children formally ask their parents to forgive them for their misdeeds. Hari Raya Haji is a quieter celebration held to honor the return from a pilgrimage to Mecca.

Buddha's birthday, Wesak Day, is celebrated nationally (pictured below). Buddhists observe the coming of Wesak Day for several weeks, with children's parties and cultural events. On the day itself, large crowds gather at temples throughout the country. They offer prayers, give alms to the monks, and release caged doves.

Among the Chinese, no festival is merrier, lasts longer, or is more universally celebrated than Chinese New Year. It goes on for fifteen days and ends with Chop Goh Mai, on a full-moon night. Dancers perform the famous lion dances through the streets and are rewarded with money wrapped in red paper packets. Families hang red lanterns and set off fireworks.

Hindu celebrations include Deepavali, Thaipusam, and Thai Ponggal. Deepavali is the Hindu festival of lights. It is a family day of new clothes, lots of food, and fun. On Deepavali, tiny oil lamps flicker all night in Hindu homes. Thaipusam (above), when penitants make a pilgrimage to Batu Caves, honors the Hindu deity Lord Subramaniam. Tamil agricultural workers celebrate Thai Ponggal, a harvest festival.

Christmas, the most widely recognized Christian holiday, is observed with big sales in the stores and midnight masses in many churches. The most enthusiastic celebrations are held in the Portuguese settlement in Melaka.

Sports and the Arts

"THE SUN NEVER SETS ON THE BRITISH EMPIRE" WAS A familiar sentence heard around the world for many decades. Colonies and protectorates governed by Great Britain did indeed stretch around the globe during the nineteenth century. Among these far-flung places was the Federated Malay States.

In 1891, an Englishman named J. Ashley Cooper suggested that various parts of the empire should come together for a pan-Britannic contest. His idea became reality in 1911, when a festival of sports was held to celebrate the coronation of King George V of England. Some years later, a Canadian named Norton Crowe proposed that the members of the British Empire get together for games of their own, to be held between the years when Olympic games were scheduled.

In 1930, Canada hosted the first British Empire Games. Eleven countries within the empire participated. Four hundred athletes competed in six sports—track and field, swimming and diving, bowling, boxing, rowing, and wrestling. At first the events were called the Friendly Games, with the stated purpose of substituting "the stimulus of novel adventure for the pleasure of international rivalry." The games should be "merrier and friendlier" than the Olympics, said the organizers.

Since 1930, these games have been held every four years, except during World War II. The name of the games changed several times, as more and more parts of the British Empire became independent nations. From 1954 to 1962 they were

Opposite: **Cyclists racing in the 1998 Commonwealth Games**

The National Sports Complex

Bukit Jalil, just south of Kuala Lumpur, is the home of a world-class sports complex. It was built to host the Commonwealth Games in 1998. Promotion of sports is one of the ways in which the Malaysian government builds national pride, and the National Sports Complex is an important reminder that Malaysia intends to be a part of international competition. Avenues of trees, fountains and pools, covered walkways, and outdoor public recreation areas surround the structures. The complex provides state-of-the-art training facilities for athletes and an excellent location for spectator-sport events.

People can take a two-hour walking tour of the National Sports Complex. The centerpiece of the complex is the National Stadium, a huge domed stadium that seats 100,000 spectators of international football games. The tour also includes the smaller Putra Stadium (which seats 16,000), the indoor and outdoor hockey stadiums, the National Aquatic Center, and the National Squash Center. Visitors can see a video of the 1998 Commonwealth Games, take in the grounds on Commonwealth Hill, and make stops at the souvenir shop and food stands. Malaysia hopes to host future Olympic games at this complex.

called the British Empire and Commonwealth Games, and from 1966 to 1974 the British Commonwealth Games. In 1978 the name of the contest was officially changed to the Commonwealth Games.

The people of Malaysia were delighted that Kuala Lumpur was chosen to host the Sixteenth Commonwealth Games in 1998. This marked the first time that the games were held in Asia. Seventy countries and territories participated, and more than 6,000 athletes and officials attended the event.

Malaysia went into high gear to get ready for the games. A huge new sports complex was built, surrounded by extensive landscaped grounds. A series of thirty-two commemorative stamps were issued between 1994 and 1998. An official mascot was chosen, Wira the Oran Utan (or orangutan). The orangutan is the only large and intelligent primate with a Malay name. A friendly and lovable animal, he was chosen to symbolize the warmth and hospitality Malaysia extends to its guests.

Rashid Sidek follows his brothers to international fame, winning a bronze medal in the 1996 Summer Olympics.

Malaysian Athletes

In 1950, Malaysian athletes began to shine at the Commonwealth Games in weightlifting. They captured two gold, three silver, and two bronze medals in that sport. In 1966, 1970, and 1974, Malaysians excelled in badminton, winning medals in men's singles, men's doubles, women's singles, and women's doubles. In the 1980s, two brothers, Razif Sidek and Jailani Sidek, became national heroes because of their prowess

Sepak Takraw

Sepak takraw, a traditional Malay game, is now recognized as Malaysia's national game. It has been played here since the fifteenth century and recognized as a modern sport since the 1930s. It resembles volleyball, with teams propelling a ball back and forth across a net. However, players cannot use hands to hit the ball. Instead, they usually kick it, although heads, elbows, and knees can also come into play.

Children learn takraw when they are quite young. It continues to be a popular recreation for adults.

in badminton. Another Malaysian, Shalin Zulkifli, was named World Bowler of the Year in 1994, at the age of 17.

Badminton and soccer (which is called football in much of the world) are the two most popular spectator sports in Malaysia. Both these sports are played by many schoolchildren from an early age. Other sports encouraged in school programs are volleyball, rugby, sepak takraw, softball, and basketball.

Malaysian sports have traditionally been promoted by voluntary organizations, but recently the government has actively encouraged physical recreation. It provides funds to assist in building sports facilities with space and programs for training. Just about every known sport, from archery to wrestling, has councils and associations.

The Arts in Malaysia

Typical Malaysian arts and crafts have a long history. Drawings and paintings that are at least 2,000 years old can be seen on the walls of caves in both West and East Malaysia. And many millennia before that, people were making pottery and creating stone carvings. Wood carving is another art that has been widely practiced in Malaysia for hundreds, if not thousands, of years. Today many arts, both traditional and modern, are flourishing in Malaysia. One of the most outstanding is architecture.

Architecture

The diversity of the Malaysian people is demonstrated in the architecture of private housing and public buildings. Colorful and elaborately decorated Chinese and Indian temples sit in the midst of simple wooden homes. Victorian-style mansions date from the British colonial days. Early mosques show traces of Dutch and Javanese influence, while modern ones have adapted styles from Western architecture.

Kuala Lumpur is a world-class showplace of the best of late twentieth-century public architecture. From the Petronas Twin Towers and the KL Tower (Menara Kuala Lumpur) to the National Stadium, the Kuala Lumpur International Airport, and the National Mosque, Malaysian modern architecture is outstanding.

Detail of a Peranakan townhouse

Traditional Malay housing was made of wood. Highly skilled carpenters and carvers created beautiful decorations on doors, windows, panels, and ceilings. Unfortunately, wood is not the most long-lived building material, and the damp, hot climate has been hard on this type of housing. Very few private homes created more than 200 years ago have been preserved. A few good examples of century-old Peranakan townhouses survive today in some of the cities, however. Various styles of longhouses are on display at the Sarawak Cultural Village near Kuching.

Badan Warisan Malaysia

Badan Warisan Malaysia is a membership organization committed to the preservation of Malaysia's architectural heritage. An example of the kind of work the group hopes to do is a restored Malay house, Rumah Penghulu, now on display in Kuala Lumpur. The building is a wonderful example of ornamental wood carving in Malay architecture.

Other Malaysian crafts are illustrated in the brasswork, weavings, and pottery used in the furnishings of the house.

Many buildings in Malaysia show the influence of the Minangkabau culture of the state of Negeri Sembilan. The outstanding feature is the shape of the roof, which sweeps upward on curved lines to a peak. It is nicknamed "buffalo horn" architecture. This feature has been used in palaces, museums, and the state legislative assembly building in Seremban.

Wood Carving

Early Malay wood-carvers went into the forests to select just the right tree to cut for their material. They would also chant magic words to appease the forest spirits who might not like to see trees cut down. Wood had a mystical importance to these artisans. They believed that certain varieties were sources of *semangat*, the life force, and that a carver would draw from that power as he worked.

Wood carving is an integral part of architecture in Malaysia. Even in today's modern steel and glass buildings, wood carvings are used for interior decoration. Wood-carvers also use their skill to build and beautify boats, and they create dozens of useful and ornamental items for everyday use and enjoyment. The Mah Meri in Selangor are known for their

Wood carving and paint ornament this fishing boat.

Children watch a traditional dance in Sabah.

wood carvings. The Iban, Kenyah, and Kayan people of Sarawak create fine hand-carved masks.

Performing Arts

Royal orchestras, called *nobat*, once performed at all ceremonial occasions in some Malay states. Only four still exist today, in the states (kingdoms) of Kedah, Terengganu, Perak, and Johor. Four or five musicians make up each combo. Their instruments are drums, flute, trumpet, and gong. *Gamelan* orchestras, once popular in Malaysia, are rare today. This style of music, introduced to Malaysia from Java, is created with gongs, xylophones, and drums. A few other types of traditional musical religious and romantic songs are still known and performed in some regions.

Traditional dances and dance dramas are popular, especially in Sabah and Sarawak. Others trace their origins to Sumatra, Thailand, China, India, Persia, and Arabia.

A new performance theater, Panggung Negara (National Theater), opened in Kuala Lumpur in the late

1990s. It is rated among the ten most sophisticated theaters in the world. Performances in this theater include chamber music, traditional and folk music, experimental programs, and concerts by the National Symphony Orchestra and the National Choir.

The Malaysian Philharmonic Orchestra gave its inaugural performance in 1998. The group includes members from twenty-two nations. It is housed in a new concert hall in the Petronas Twin Towers. The hall is designed with movable acoustical devices so that volume and resonance can be adjusted as needed.

Literature

Only since independence have Malaysians throughout the nation been encouraged to learn and use one official language—Bahasa Malaysia. Before that, the use of many languages and dialects in different parts of the nation prevented the development of a national literature. The government is promoting Malaysian literature (written in Bahasa Malaysia) through a number of programs. The Institute of Language and Literature works to standardize rules of spelling and grammar, publishes Malaysian works, and promotes local literary talent. The National Library of Malaysia collects books, periodicals, and manuscripts about Malaysia and directs programs to promote reading.

People around the world have learned about the Malay Peninsula through novels written by British writers. Joseph Conrad wrote *Lord Jim*; *Victory, an Island Tale*; and *The Rescue*, for example. Later, W. Somerset Maugham, another Englishman, wrote of British colonial life in *Malaysian Stories*. Even earlier, in the 1870s, Isabella Bird, a traveler from England, wrote detailed descriptions of her own journeys in the Malay states in *The Golden Chersonese*. Her vivid descriptions of the people and their daily lives, the landscape, and her own adventures provide a close look at this country as it was in the nineteenth century.

Painting

The Craft Cultural Center in Kuala Lumpur is the home of the National Art Gallery, a group of shops featuring Malaysian handicrafts and several artists' studios. Here some eighteen resident artists work and display their products for sale.

The National Art Gallery was established in 1958. It now has its own modern building and a collection of several thousand works selected to reflect the spirit and personality of the nation. Art is displayed in three galleries. The first floor is used for pieces selected from the museum's permanent collection. The second floor houses temporary exhibits of both Malaysian and foreign works. The Creative Gallery, where a variety of experimental works are shown, is on the third floor.

Traditional Handicrafts

Malay sultans, princes, and nobility were the principal supporters of local artisans in earlier times. Even 2,000 years ago, Malay was famous for the gold jewelry and gold-threaded clothing worn by its royalty and their courts.

The crafts of metalwork, wood carving, and weaving have been preserved, especially on the peninsula's east coast. Designs incorporate motifs from nature—flowers, leaves, feathers, butterflies. Some of the designs probably originated during the early Indian period. Islam, which later became the accepted religion, forbids any depiction of the human form in artwork.

Metalwork is created in several parts of Sarawak. Fine, delicate silverware is produced in Kelantan; workers in Terengganu specialize in white brass.

Royal Selangor Pewter

Royal Selangor pewter is manufactured in a suburb of Kuala Lumpur. Pewter is a shiny metal similar to silver, made from antimony, copper, and refined tin. Unlike silver, it doesn't tarnish. Royal Selangor tea sets, picture frames, boxes, trays, and other decorative items are exported throughout the world.

Making labu sayong

Pack baskets used to carry heavy loads in Sarawak

The village of Sayong, in Perak, is famous for its pottery, called *labu sayong*, or "Sayong pumpkins." This craft has been handed down among generations of women. Traditional pottery is a major industry in Sarawak, and several potteries in Sabah produce utilitarian and ornamental glazed pottery.

Nomadic people in Sabah and Sarawak create fine baskets and hats from split rattan. They find rattan deep in the forests, and then they dry, split, and color it with dyes made of forest leaves. Rattan is a climbing palm tree with very long, tough stems. Leaves of the pandanus (screw pine) tree and the fronds of the nipa palm are also used for weaving fine mats. Mats are used as floor or bed coverings, at the beach, and to spread out food for drying.

A person weaving a mat begins in the center and moves outward. Crisscross or hexagonal patterns are common, but some weavers design more elaborate patterns. In addition to mats, many other products of *pandan* weaving are crafted all over the country.

Hand-crafted decorative shields and handles for swords, spears, and especially the keris (Malaysian daggers) are important symbols of Malaysia's heritage. Many of these are examples of superior craftsmanship.

Woven silk brocade cloth, called *kain songket*, has been made in Malaysia for many generations. Elaborate silk brocade garments are worn for royal ceremonies, weddings, and other important occasions. Certain designs are reserved for use only by royalty. Traditionally, the best weavers were chosen among hundreds of women and given the honor of working for the palace.

Often, nobles create their own designs. One well-known workshop is headed by a Terengganu prince. Terengganu and Kelantan are the weaving centers of the country. The looms and techniques used today are the same as in the old days. The center panel of a length of cloth, called the *kepala*, has the most elaborate pattern.

Tekat is gold embroidery on dark velvet cloth. Another distinctive woven cloth that uses a tie-dyed warp, called ikat, is made by the Iban people of Sarawak.

Batik cloth is Malaysia's most popular fabric craft. To a great extent, batik is thought of as typical of the Malaysian culture. The textile is used for formal shirts, sarongs, and the traditional women's dress called *baju kurung*. Most Malaysian batik is produced on the east coast of the peninsula.

Batik

The art of making batik cloth originated in Indonesia and was brought to Malaysia in the 1930s. Patterns are stamped onto cloth with metal printing blocks or are hand-drawn with a wax-filled penlike instrument. Then the dye is painted onto the cloth with brushes. The most skillful artisans draw the patterns freehand rather than using printing blocks.

Growing Up
in Malaysia

THE FIRST WORDS A NEWBORN MALAY CHILD HEARS ARE the Muslim call to prayer. As soon as an infant is bathed and wrapped in cloth, the father takes it in his arms and whispers the sacred words in the child's ear. A week later, relatives gather to witness the official naming of the baby.

In the kampungs, young children are loved and pampered by older members of the family and neighbors. Adults often stop their own activities to take care of or play with youngsters.

Malaysian children start school when they are six years old. Malay-language schools are open to all communities, but Chinese and Indian communities often have their own schools. All children are taught to speak Bahasa Malaysia, the national language. However, Chinese and Indian schools teach it as a second language, using the native language of the ethnic group for other subjects. Very few children in some big cities attend private, expensive, English-language schools. All schoolchildren wear the uniform of their school—usually a white shirt and dark trousers for boys, and a traditional long skirt and loose top or a modern blouse and pinafore for girls.

Opposite: **Muslim children in a classroom**

Schoolboys in uniform

Traditional Games

Some games and sports played by both children and adults in Malaysia have been known in this part of the world for hundreds of years. Malaysian children, especially those who live in rural regions, are very resourceful in their play. They use natural objects such as seeds and sticks in place of marbles and manufactured game pieces to play a number of games.

Top-spinning (pictured) is a highly skilled competitive sport in some villages. In many regions, kite-flying is far more than a pastime; it is an occasion for inter-national festivals. Handmade kites are works of superior artistic and engineering skill.

Sepak takraw, a game something like volleyball, is popular in several Asian countries. Congkak is a board game of many variations and names in different parts of the world. Toy stores in the United States sell it under the name Mancala.

Asian self-defense sports, such as kendo, tae kwon do, and judo, are popular in Malaysia. Certain forms practiced by Malays and bumiputras are called *silat*.

Many Chinese children start kindergarten at three or four and begin to learn arithmetic and a few written characters. When they are a little older, they are expected to help with household chores, working with their parents on the family farm or in the family store.

A Malaysian home may be a small riverside stilt house, a sultan's palace, a modern government-built apartment in a city or a suburban area, a Chinese shop-house, or a small row house on an oil-palm plantation. In any case, it is an extended-family refuge where relatives are always welcome for short or long visits. It is where people come together to share important experiences, whether they are happy or sad occasions. Village people who have moved to the city hurry back to the kampung to celebrate festivals. Family life is at the center of every aspect of Malaysian life.

A traditional Malay kampung house is built of wood, with a small roofed patio outside the front door. (Visitors leave their shoes here before entering.) The house may be on one floor, be a split-level with bedrooms upstairs, or consist of two or two-and-a-half stories. If the house has more than one floor, the ground level is used for storage, and an outside flight of stairs leads to the main living quarters. A carved railing encloses a small deck. The design is planned to capture breezes and keep the rooms as cool as possible. Shuttered windows surround large, high-ceilinged rooms. Wide sloping roofs protect the interior from direct sunlight. Gardens, potted plants, and trees surround the chaletlike building.

Many traditional houses are built of wood.

The veranda of an Iban longhouse

Chinese merchant families usually live in shop-houses. Their stores are on the first floor, and the living quarters are above. Some of the loveliest townhouses in Malaysia date to the days when wealthy Chinese merchants began to settle down on the peninsula and married local Malay women. These families of mixed heritage were known as Peranakans, or Straits Chinese, or Baba-Nonyas. Melaka has a cluster of their seventeenth-century townhouses; a few others are in Pulau Pinang. The original owners filled the large, airy rooms with expensive imported furniture. Gilded picture frames, chests inlaid with marble and mother-of-pearl, and intricately carved doors were all symbols of the wealth of the owners.

Many of the people of Sarawak lived in unusual quarters called longhouses. Some still do, although there are fewer of them. In a way, longhouses can be thought of as early versions of modern condominiums. Several families occupy separate living quarters under one roof, under the leadership of a chief or a headman. The long wooden structure is a series of large rooms that all open onto a wide and long veranda. Longhouse roofs used to be made of palm-leaf thatch; today corrugated iron is more commonly used. Each room belongs to a family; they eat and sleep here. Social activities take place on the veranda or in other parts of the village.

Marriage Customs

Arranged marriages are still quite common in Malay and Indian communities, less so among the Chinese. Of course, young people today have more opportunities to know people of the opposite sex than many of their elders did. Often they have ideas of their own about whom they'd like to marry. Legally, Malaysians younger than twenty-one cannot marry without their parents' consent. On the other hand, they cannot be forced to marry against their will.

The parents of a young Indian girl will tell her that an arranged marriage is better because they can protect her if problems arise. However, if she goes off on her own, they wouldn't be able to help. Even if a young man and woman have made up their own minds, they may want their parents to get together and "arrange" the match. Hindu weddings are splendid spectacles, traditionally held in temples.

Muslims have strict rules about mixed marriages. Religious law forbids a Muslim woman to marry a non-Muslim man, unless he converts to Islam. A Muslim

man can marry a non-Muslim, but unless his wife converts, she cannot inherit his property or be guardian of her own children in case of his death.

A marriage tradition among Malays that predates Islamic times is for a couple to sit in state, dressed in finery, as "monarchs for a day." Some young people choose to color their feet and hands with a reddish dye called henna.

People who live in longhouses are farmers who raise crops for local consumption and sale. Many of the women are talented weavers.

Clothing

What do Malaysians wear? That depends on what ethnic group they belong to and where they live. Most Malay businessmen who live in the cities wear the same kinds of shirts and trousers to work as do most men who live in New York or London. Some of the time they may wear a *baja*, a loose Malaysian shirt, over their trousers.

Some Malay women and girls choose to wear a veil.

An article of clothing that is very useful for both men and women is the *sarung*, or sarong, as it is spelled in English. It is a straight piece of cloth that is wrapped around the body in various fashions and draped to fall in graceful folds. A woman's sarong is made to reach from the shoulder to the floor; a man's is shorter. A man will wear his tied around his waist and over his trousers. Muslim girls and women, if they choose to, wear the *tudung*, or veil. It is not mandatory, but it has become increasingly popular in recent years. The Malay veil does not cover the face; it is a silk scarf that is fastened tightly over the hair and under the chin and falls to about elbow-length.

Muslims cover their heads when they go to prayers. Men may wear a special hat at prayers called a *songkok*.

Most Malaysian Chinese wear western clothes, from casual sports clothes to the most elegant high-fashion designs, depending on the occasion. Some women wear a cotton trouser suit, but this seems to be going out of fashion. Until recently, Chinese never wore black except to funerals, but this too is no longer the rule. On rare occasions, Chinese people will dress up in elaborate costumes of earlier days.

Blue jeans, short skirts, and other Western clothes do not appeal to most older Indian women. Teenaged girls may want to follow current international fashions, but their mothers and aunts prefer the traditional *sari* and *coli* (a short blouse worn under the sari). Indian men wear western clothes except on festive occasions or for visits to temple. Then some of them wear a short sarong, called a *dhoti*, with a white cotton shirt.

People in the interior of East Malaysia follow a variety of traditions in clothing. For example, in the remote parts of Sabah, clothing is traditionally black and often trimmed with beads and gold and silver braids. The women usually wear coiled brass necklaces, anklets, and bracelets.

Good Manners

In Malay society, the first rule of proper behavior is to give respect and obedience to one's parents and other elders. Villages depend on neighborliness and community self-help, called *gotong-royong*. Law and order in the village is maintained through cooperation with and respect for the village leaders.

Malaysian Satay

Mix together:

    1 tsp cumin seeds

    1 tsp coriander seeds

    1 tsp turmeric powder

    10 shallots, diced

    1 tsp sugar

    1 tsp cinnamon

    2 tsp cooking oil

Cut a pound of chicken into bite-size pieces. Marinate the pieces in the oil and seasonings, then thread them onto skewers and grill over a charcoal fire. When cooked, serve them with onion and cucumber slices and peanut sauce.

    Peanut sauce:

    1 cup unsalted peanuts, ground

    2 stalks lemon grass

    1 piece ginger

    3 ground red chilies

    2 tsp cooking oil

    1 cup tamerind juice

    1 cup coconut milk

Westerners who visit Malaysia should be aware that certain things taken for granted at home would be regarded as very bad manners in this country. For example, one should never touch another person, even a child. It is rude to point at a person with the hand or to sit with crossed legs so that the toes point at another person. Kissing in public, even if it is a child or a baby, is very much frowned upon.

Food

Food is an important part of holiday celebrations in Malaysia. During Ramadan, the Muslim holy month, followers of Islam are forbidden to eat anything during daylight hours. After sundown, hundreds of food vendors appear on the streets of every village and town, selling Malaysian fast foods. One of the most popular is *satay*, bite-size pieces of skewered meat cooked over a charcoal fire and served with a spicy peanut sauce.

When Ramadan ends, Hari Raya Puasa is a nonstop food festival. Families, neighbors, and friends gather in one another's homes and choose from an array of dozens of dishes. *Nasi* (rice) and *mee* (noodles) are served in countless combinations with meat, fish, fowl, bits of vegetables, and hot spices.

Curry powder—usually mixed at home according to individual recipes—is a popular ingredient, as is coconut milk.

The different religions practiced in Malaysia have different food taboos. Muslims do not eat pork, and other meats must be *halal* (kosher), meaning that they were slaughtered according to religious dietary laws. Most Hindus and Sikhs eat no beef, and some are vegetarians.

Tropical Fruits

You may have seen starfruit in a specialty grocery market, but can you identify a rambutan, a mangosteen, a cempedak, a ciku, or a durian? The starfruit (pictured on the right) has soft yellow flesh, and its juice is sweet, with just a hint of sourness. A rambutan has red or yellow skin and white flesh. It tastes a little like a lychee. You have tasted a lychee, haven't you?

The mangosteen (above) has purple skin and white, juicy flesh. A cempedak has a scaly, greenish yellow skin. The segments of fruit have large seeds that can be eaten. A ciku looks a little like a kiwi.

The durian is an infamous fruit. The fruit is large, with a soft cheeselike flesh wrapped around a very big seed. Those who are used to it think it is delicious, but strangers usually are reluctant to try it because it smells rotten!

Fish and shellfish, plentiful in Malaysian waters, are naturally used a great deal. So are the many fruits from the tropical forests. Some of these, very common in that part of the world, are nearly unknown in faraway parts of the world.

Restaurants in the cities reflect the ethnic variety of the Malaysian population. Chinese restaurants serve dishes from many Chinese provinces. Indian eateries usually specialize in the hot, spicy dishes from southern India or the milder ones from the north. Indian "banana leaf" restaurants serve food on circles of banana leaves instead of plates.

Restaurants serve all types of food.

Vegetarians can find both Chinese and Indian vegetarian restaurants in Malaysia. Even British and other European residents have added their influence to Malaysian eating habits. Sometimes the combinations are quite surprising. For instance, can you imagine a curried pizza? And Malaysian youngsters are quite familiar with hamburgers—which are generally called "beefburgers" to emphasize that they do not contain pork.

According to gourmets, the finest cuisine in the country is the one that has been handed down in the Peranakan culture—consisting of typical Chinese ingredients prepared with Malay spices, along with a suggestion of Thai influence.

The people of East Malaysia have traditionally eaten many meats and fish that are unfamiliar to most outsiders. But today they often use Chinese soy sauce and Malay spices in preparing game animals for dinner.

Malaysia's Future

As a nation, Malaysia's aims are clear. Its leaders are committed to developing it into one of the fully industrialized nations of the world by the year 2020. It has already outstripped its neighbors (Indonesia, the Philippines, Thailand, Vietnam, and China) in several measurable ways. The life expectancy rate is the highest in the region, and the infant mortality rate the lowest. The Malaysian population ranks high in having all the tools necessary for the Information Age. Malaysians have more newspapers, radios, telephones, mobile phones, fax machines, and personal computers per capita than any of its

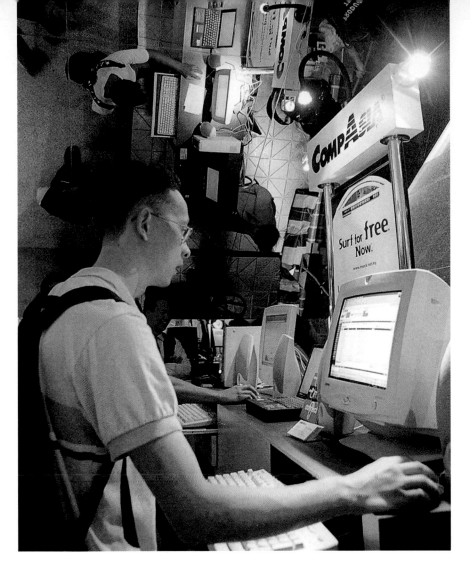

Checking e-mail in Kuala Lumpur

neighbors, and they are second only to Thais in ownership of television sets.

Malaysia's goals go beyond physical assets, however. The country has made great gains in modernizing its industry and infrastructure. If it can do as much to improve the quality of life for all its citizens—who represent so many ethnic groups, religions, and economic levels—it will rapidly become a model for other nations to follow.

Timeline

Malaysian History

People are living in caves in Sarawak.	**About** 38000 B.C.
People are living on the Malay Peninsula.	**About** 8000 B.C.
People from southern China are living on the Malay Peninsula.	**About** 1000 B.C.
Melaka becomes a trading center on the Malay Peninsula.	**About** A.D. 1400
Melaka becomes an Islamic kingdom, and Islam spreads throughout the peninsula.	1450s
Portuguese take control of Melaka.	1511
United East India Company gains control of Melaka.	1640
The British gain control of Pulau Pinang and Melaka.	1785–1824

World History

2500 B.C.	Egyptians build the Pyramids and the Sphinx in Giza.
563 B.C.	The Buddha is born in India.
A.D. 313	The Roman emperor Constantine recognizes Christianity.
610	The Prophet Muhammad begins preaching a new religion called Islam.
1054	The Eastern (Orthodox) and Western (Roman) Churches break apart.
1066	William the Conqueror defeats the English in the Battle of Hastings.
1095	Pope Urban II proclaims the First Crusade.
1215	King John seals the Magna Carta.
1300s	The Renaissance begins in Italy.
1347	The Black Death sweeps through Europe.
1453	Ottoman Turks capture Constantinople, conquering the Byzantine Empire.
1492	Columbus arrives in North America.
1500s	The Reformation leads to the birth of Protestantism.
1776	The Declaration of Independence is signed.
1789	The French Revolution begins.

Malaysian History

The British Brooke family rules Sarawak with permission from the sultan of Brunei.	1846–1941
The British North Borneo Company rules Sabah.	1881–1946
North Borneo and Sarawak become British protectorates.	1888
Britain controls all of what is now peninsular Malaysia.	1914
Japan occupies British Malaya during World War II.	1941–1945
Britain forms the Malayan Union.	1946
The Federation of Malaya is formed.	1948
The Federation of Malaya gains independence from Britain.	1957
The nation of Malaysia is formed.	1963
Riots break out between Chinese and Malays.	1969
The government begins a twenty-year plan called the New Economic Policy.	1970
Petronas Twin Towers, the world's tallest building, is completed in Kuala Lumpur.	1996
Kuala Lumpur International Airport opens in Sepang.	1998
Putrajaya becomes the administrative capital of Malaysia.	2000

World History

1865	The American Civil War ends.
1914	World War I breaks out.
1917	The Bolshevik Revolution brings communism to Russia.
1929	Worldwide economic depression begins.
1939	World War II begins, following the German invasion of Poland.
1945	World War II ends.
1957	The Vietnam War starts.
1969	Humans land on the moon.
1975	The Vietnam War ends.
1979	Soviet Union invades Afghanistan.
1983	Drought and famine in Africa.
1989	The Berlin Wall is torn down as communism crumbles in Eastern Europe.
1991	Soviet Union breaks into separate states.
1992	Bill Clinton is elected U.S. president.
2000	George W. Bush is elected U.S. president.

Fast Facts

Official name: Malaysia

Capital: Kuala Lumpur; administrative capital, Putrajaya

Official language: Bahasa Malaysia

Kuala Lumpur

Malaysia's flag

Ranger with young
orangutans

Official religion:	Islam
Year of founding:	1963
National anthem:	"Negara Ku" ("My Country")
Government:	Federal constitutional monarchy
Chief of state:	Yang di-Pertuan Agong (paramount ruler)
Head of government:	Prime minister
Area:	128,525 square miles (332,878 sq km)
Greatest length:	670 miles (1,078 km) in East Malaysia
Greatest width:	240 miles (386 km) in East Malaysia
Latitude and longitude of geographic center:	30° 2' north latitude, 30° 112' east longitude
Neighboring countries:	Thailand, Singapore, Indonesia, and Brunei
Water borders:	Straits of Malacca, South China Sea, Sulu Sea, Celebes Sea
Highest elevation:	Mount Kinabalu, 13,431 feet (4,094 m) above sea level
Lowest elevation:	Sea level, along the coast
Average temperature extremes:	90°F (32°C) along the coasts; 55°F (13°C) in the mountains
Average precipitation extremes:	150 inches (381 cm) in Sarawak and Sabah; 100 inches (254 cm) on the Malaysian Peninsula
National population (1999 est.):	21,329,000

Petronas Twin Towers

Currency

Population of largest cities (1991 est):		
	Kuala Lumpur	1,145,342
	Ipoh	382,853
	Johor Baharu	328,436
	Melaka	296,897
	Petaling Jaya	254,350

Famous landmarks:
- ▶ **Batu Caves**, north of Kuala Lumpur
- ▶ **Gunung Mulu National Park**, Sarawak
- ▶ **Kellie's Castle**, south of Ipoh
- ▶ **Kinabalu Park and Mount Kinabalu**, Sabah
- ▶ **Lake Gardens**, Kuala Lumpur
- ▶ **Niah Caves**, Sarawak
- ▶ **Penang Museum**, George Town
- ▶ **Petronas Twin Towers**, Kuala Lumpur
- ▶ **Sarawak Museum**, Kuching
- ▶ **Sepilok Orang-utan Rehabilitation Center**, Sabah
- ▶ **Sungai Palas Tea Estate**, Cameron Highlands

Industry: Manufacturing and service industries employ most of Malaysia's nonagricultural workers. Many of them work in the electronics industry making integrated circuits. Other factory workers build Malaysia's own automobile, the Proton. Malaysia's service industries sell goods in stores, move goods throughout the country, and run Malaysia's government. Tourism is a fast-growing industry that earns several billion dollars each year.

Currency: The basic unit of currency in Malaysia is the ringgit (RM). As of May 2001, US$1 equaled RM 3.75.

System of weights and measures: The metric system is the standard system of weights and measures, with some use of British imperial units.

Malaysian children

Literacy (1999): 94 percent

Common Malaysian words and phrases:

Apa khabar? (apa khabar)	Hello/How are you?
Bagaimana saya pergi ki . . . ? (ba-gai-ma-na sa-ya per-gee-ke)	How do I get to . . . ?
Harganya berapa? (HAR-ga-nya ber-A-pa)	How much does it cost?
Maafkan saya. (ma-fkan sa-ya)	Excuse me.
Sila. (SEE-la)	Please.
Terima kasih. (TREE-ma KA-say)	Thank you.
Tidak. (TEE-dak)	No.
Tolong! (TO-long)	Help!
Ya. (ya)	Yes.

Famous People:

James Brooke (1803–1868)
First white rajah of Sarawak, from 1846 to 1868

Charles Johnson Brooke (1829–1917)
Second white rajah of Sarawak, from 1868 to 1917

Ibrahim Hussein (1936–)
Abstract artist

Mahathir bin Mohamad (1925–)
Prime minister from 1978 to the present

Paramesvara (1370–1460)
Founder and ruler of Melaka

Tunku Abdul Rahman (1903–1990)
Malaya's and Malaysia's first prime minister, from 1957–1970

Abdul Samad Said (1935–)
Writer

Mahathir bin Mohamad

To Find Out More

Books

▶ Bird, Isabella. *The Golden Chersonese*. Koln, Germany: Konemann Travel Classics, 2000 edition.

▶ Bratvold, Gretchen (ed). *Malaysia in Pictures*. Minneapolis: Visual Geography Series, Lerner Publications Company, 1989.

▶ Brooke, Margaret, the Ranee of Sarawak. *My Life in Sarawak*. Singapore and New York: Oxford University Press, 1998.

▶ Major, John S. *The Land and People of Malaysia & Brunei*. New York: Portraits of the Nations Series, HarperCollins, 1991.

▶ Munan, Heidi. *Culture Shock! Malaysia*. Singapore and Kuala Lumpur: Times Books International: 1991.

▶ Munan, Heidi. *Malaysia*. New York: Cultures of the World series, Marshall Cavendish, 1990.

▶ Rowell, Jonathan. *Malaysia*. Austin, TX: Economically Developing Countries, Raintree Steck-Vaughn Company, 1997.

Websites

▶ **Malaysia**
www.geographia.com/malaysia/
Information about the people, places, history, nature, activities, travel, and calendar of events in Malaysia.

▶ **The CIA World Factbook**
www.odci.gov/cia/publications/
factbook/geos/my.html
Updated information, maps, and facts on geography, people, and more.

▶ **Tourism Malaysia**
www.tourism.gov.my
Information about travel to Malaysia.

Organizations and Embassies

▶ **Tourism Malaysia**
595 Madison Ave., Suite 1800
New York, NY 10022

▶ **Diplomatic Representative of Malaysia in the United States**
2401 Massachusetts Ave., N.W.
Washington, DC 20008

▶ **Permanent Mission of Malaysia to the United Nations**
313 East 43rd Street
New York, NY 10017

Index

Page numbers in *italics* indicate illustrations.

Meet the Author

SYLVIA MCNAIR was born in Korea and believes she inherited a love of travel from her missionary parents. She grew up in Vermont. After graduating from Oberlin College, she held a variety of jobs, married, had four children, and settled in the Chicago area. She now lives in Evanston, Illinois. She is the author of several travel guides and more than twenty books for young people published by Children's Press.

"Every country in the world is fascinating once you start to find out about it. I have always been especially interested in Asian countries, because their civilization goes so far back in history. Several Malaysian cities were ports of call to travelers from dozens of other countries long before explorers from Europe knew anything about the Western Hemisphere.

"Rapid communication and transportation is making the world seem so much smaller. That's why it is important to learn about other countries. E-mail makes it as easy to stay in touch with people halfway around the world as with those in the next town.

"Malaysia is not a very large country, in population. But it is one of the most diverse societies anywhere. Dozens of ethnic groups and languages, many religions and beliefs, millions of animal and plant species, a varied terrain—all of these things make Malaysia a great place to visit or to explore by reading. I hope you will enjoy learning about it."

McNair has traveled in more than forty countries and in all fifty of the United States.

Photo Credits

Photographs ©:

AP/Wide World Photos: 100 (Frank Gunn), 103 (Kastumi Kasahara), 99 right, 127 (Teh Eng Koon), 99 left (Peter Liew), 52, 54 (Vincent Thian), 53, 58 (Andy Wong), 23, 55

Archive Photos/Getty Images/Chai Hin Goh/Reuters: 64

Bridgeman Art Library International Ltd./ London Zoological Society, UK: 42

Bruce Coleman Inc.: 13, 15, 62, 89, 92 (Massimo Borchi), 34 (Eric Hosking), 20 (Karen McGougan)

Corbis Images: 49, 133 bottom (AFP), 84 (Dave Bartruff), 46, 48 top (Bettmann), 9, 10 top, 97, 132 top (Eye Ubiquitous), 107 (Dave G. Houser), 7 bottom, 74 (Wolfgang Kaehler), 114, 119 (Earl & Nazima Kowall), 106 (Bob Krist), 50, 93 (Charles & Josette Lenars), 77 (Neil Rabinowitz), 91 (Steve Raymer), 60, 112 top (Reuters NewMedia Inc.), 73, 102 (Paul Russell), 83 (Robert van der Hilst), cover, 6, 38, 86, 108 (Nik Wheeler)

Dave G. Houser/HouserStock, Inc.: 76 bottom, 133 top (Neil Montanus), 40, 57 left, 111

Hulton Archive/Getty Images: 47 (Central Press), 45 (Illustrated London News)

International Stock Photo/Jeff Greenberg: 63

MapQuest.com, Inc.: 56, 131 top

Minden Pictures: 33 top (Gerry Ellis), 7 top, 12, 21 top, 28, 29 top, 30, 31, 131 bottom (Frans Lanting)

Network Aspen: 72 (Paul Chesley), 68, 117 (Nicholas Devore III), 87, 112 bottom (David Hiser), 21 bottom, 35 (Jones & Shimlock)

Peter Arnold Inc.: 22 top (T. Domico/ Bios), 24 (Michael J. Doolittle), 82 (Jeff Greenberg), 69 top (Lineair), 69 bottom (D. Novellino/Still Pictures)

Photo Researchers, NY: 17 top (Alain Evrard), 33 bottom (Fletcher & Baylis), 25 (Tom McHugh/Steinhart Aquarium), 22 bottom, 32 (Simon D. Pollard), 115 (Jim Steinberg), 29 bottom (Dr. Paul Zahl)

Portfolio Group/Jim Steinberg: 43, 71, 132 bottom

Robert & Linda Mitchell: 18, 57 right, 81, 95

Robert Fried Photography: 78, 113, 123, 125

Stone/Getty Images/Hans Strand: 8

Superstock, Inc.: 94 (Bibliotheque Nationale, Paris/Bridgeman Art Library, London), 118 (Robin Smith), 2, 10 bottom, 17 bottom, 61 top, 65, 88, 130 left

The Image Works/M. Granitsas: 120

Viesti Collection, Inc./Walter Bibikow: 67

Visuals Unlimited: 124 top (George Loun), 37 (Ken Lucas), 124 bottom (David Sieren), 27 (Richard Thom)

Woodfin Camp & Associates: 116 (David Alan Harvey), 104 (Kal Muller)

Maps by Joe LeMonnier